SMP interact

Book 1

W9-BNT-004

1

CAMBRIDGE
UNIVERSITY PRESS

PUBLISHED BY THE PRESS SYNDICATE OF THE UNIVERSITY OF CAMBRIDGE
The Pitt Building, Trumpington Street, Cambridge, United Kingdom

CAMBRIDGE UNIVERSITY PRESS
The Edinburgh Building, Cambridge CB2 2RU, UK   http://www.cup.cam.ac.uk
40 West 20th Street, New York, NY 10011–4211, USA   http://www.cup.org
10 Stamford Road, Oakleigh, Melbourne 3166, Australia
Ruiz de Alarcón 13, 28014 Madrid, Spain

© The School Mathematics Project 2000
First published 2000

Printed in the United Kingdom at the University Press, Cambridge

Typeface Minion   *System* QuarkXPress®

A catalogue record for this book is available from the British Library

ISBN 0 521 77795 X paperback

Illustrations by Robert Calow and Steve Lach at Eikon Illustration and Jeff Edwards
Handwriting by Hilary Evans
Cover image by Eikon Illustration
Cover design by Angela Ashton

The publishers would like to thank the following for supplying photographs:
page 36   Guraj N Sharma / DPA / Images of India
page 73   London Transport Museum
page 102   Tony Stone Images
page 169   Popperfoto/Reuters
page 182   The J Allan Cash Photolibrary
page 183   John Ling
page 189   Tony Stone Images
All other photographs by Graham Portlock

The publishers would like to thank the following for permission to use their logo:
page 29 question C2(j) National Westminster Bank

The authors and publishers would like to thank the staff and pupils of The
Netherhall School, Cambridge, for their help with the production of this book.

NOTICE TO TEACHERS
It is illegal to reproduce any part of this work in material form (including photocopying
and electronic storage) except under the following circumstances:
(i) where you are abiding by a licence granted to your school by the Copyright Licensing Agency;
(ii) where no such licence exists, or where you wish to exceed the terms of a licence, and you
have gained the written permission of Cambridge University Press;
(iii) where you are allowed to reproduce without permission under the provisions of Chapter 3
of the Copyright, Designs and Patents Act 1988.

Contents

S1 Spot the mistake *Miss S1*

You need sheets 45 and 46.

Each picture contains errors.
Some are mathematical, some are not.

How many can you find?

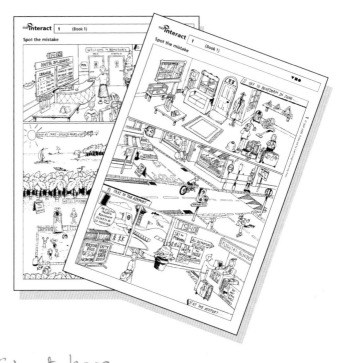

S2 Four digits *Start here*

The class chooses four digits, for example

1, 2, 3, 4

Try to make as many numbers from 1 to 100 as possible.
Use the four digits and any signs you want.

$$1 + 2 + 3 + 4 = 10$$

$$13 + 4 - 2 = 15$$

S3 Two-piece tangrams

1 Rectangle

Start with a rectangle 7 cm by 4 cm.
Draw a diagonal.

You will need several copies.

Cut them out. Cut along the diagonal.

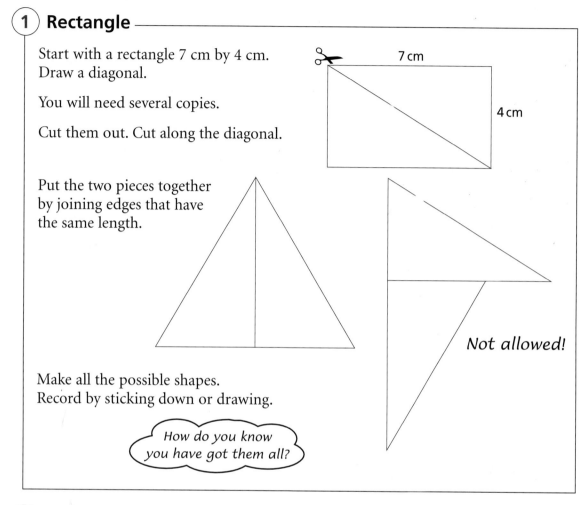

Put the two pieces together
by joining edges that have
the same length.

Make all the possible shapes.
Record by sticking down or drawing.

*How do you know
you have got them all?*

Not allowed!

2 Square

Start with a square.

Join the midpoint of one side to an opposite corner.

You will need several copies.

Cut out and cut along the slanting line.

Put the pieces together. Join edges that are the same length.

Make all the possible shapes.
How do you know you have got them all?

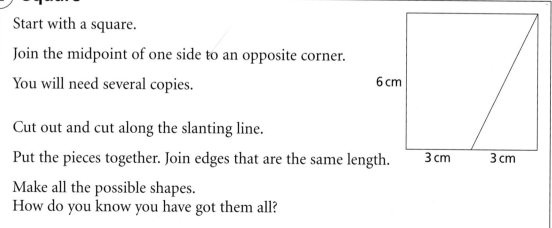

S4 Lunch break

You need a copy of your school lunch menu with prices.

How much do these cost in your school? *Miss*

1

Pizza, chips and an apple

2

Jacket potato with
baked beans and salad

3

Orange juice,
cheese and tomato
sandwich, cake

4 Choose five meals of your own. *Miss*
Ask someone else to work out what each meal costs.
Check their adding.

5
> I had £2.50.
> I spent £1.15.
>
> How much money
> did I have left?

6
> I had £3.00.
> I spent £1.35.
>
> How much money
> did I have left?

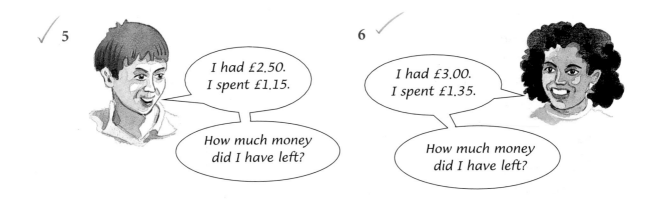

7 Make up five questions of your own, like questions 5 and 6.
Ask someone else to do them. Check their answers.

8 Make a poster to show a meal which costs between £1 and £1.50.

9 Solve these menu puzzles.

a

Tea	35p
Tea and bun	58p
Tea, bun and jam	75p
Tea, bun, jam and cream	99p
Bun, jam and cream	?
Bun and cream	?

b

Samosa	45p
Samosa and onion bhaji	98p
Samosa, onion bhaji and relish	£1.39
Samosa and relish	?
Onion bhaji and relish	?

c

Pie	75p
Pie and chips	£1.42
Pie and onions	£1.23
Pie and beans	£1.37
Pie, chips and onions	?
Pie, chips, onions and beans	?
Beans and chips	?

d

Egg and tomato	80p
Egg and beans	71p
Beans and tomato	65p
Egg, beans and tomato	?

e

Sausage and chips	£1.35
Sausage and egg	£1.49
Egg and chips	£1.10
Sausage, egg and chips	?

S5 Finding your way

A Left and right

A1 Bob is looking at a map.
Which hand is he holding it with?

A2 Julie is pointing.
Which hand is she pointing with?

A3 Asad is holding the dog's lead.
Which hand is he holding it with?

A4 Which ear is the dog scratching?

A5 Sandra and Peter are holding hands.
Which of Peter's hands is Sandra holding?

A6 Which of Sandra's hands is Peter holding?

A7 Arjan is doing a cartwheel.
Which of his hands is on the ground?

A8 Rob lives at the shop.
· · · · · shows the way he goes to school.
He passes the post office on his left.
What else does he see on his left on the way to school?

A9 Ann lives at Wood Farm.
– – – shows the way she goes to school.
Which roads does she use on her way to school?

A10 A visitor at the hotel asks you the way to the bank.
What would you say?

A11 Imagine that you live at the Red House in Town Road.
Describe how you would get to school.

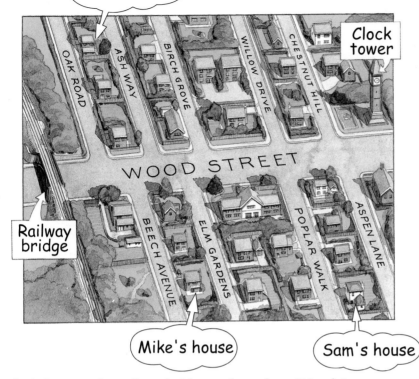

A12 Start at the railway bridge and go along Wood Street.
Oak Road is the **first turning** on your left.
We say **first left**.

Which turnings are these?

(a) Ash Way   (b) Beech Avenue   (c) Poplar Walk

(d) Chestnut Hill   (e) Aspen Lane

A13 Start at the clock tower. Go along Wood Street towards
the railway bridge.

(a) Which is the first turning on your left?

(b) Which is the third right?

(c) Which turning is Beech Avenue?

A14 Find Mike's house in Beech Avenue.
From Mike's house describe how you would get to
Sam's house in Poplar Walk.

A15 From Sam's house, describe how you would get to
Nikki's house in Oak Road.

B Reading a map

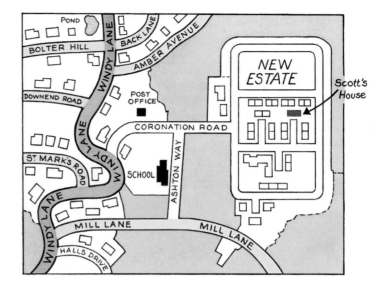

B1 Find the pond on the map.
You start at the pond
and walk along Windy Lane.

(a) Which is the first
turning on your left?

(b) Which is the second on
your right?

(c) You turn into
Coronation Road. Is the
post office on the left
side or the right side of
the road?

(d) You pass the post office and turn into Ashton Way.
Do you turn left or right?

(e) You walk along Ashton Way.
Is the school on your left or your right?

(f) You stop at Mill Lane, turn round and go back along
Ashton Way.
Which side is the school on, left or right?

B2 You are back by the pond in Windy Lane.
Someone asks you the way to the post office.
What would you say?

B3 Find Scott's house.
The roads on the new estate do not have names yet.
Describe how you would get to Scott's house from the school.

B4 This is a picture of the school.
Which roads can you see in the picture?

B5 On the map below, start at Lark Cottage and follow these directions. Where do you finish?

> Turn right.
> Go straight on at the crossroads.
> Straight on at the next crossroads.
> Second left.
> First right.
> First left.

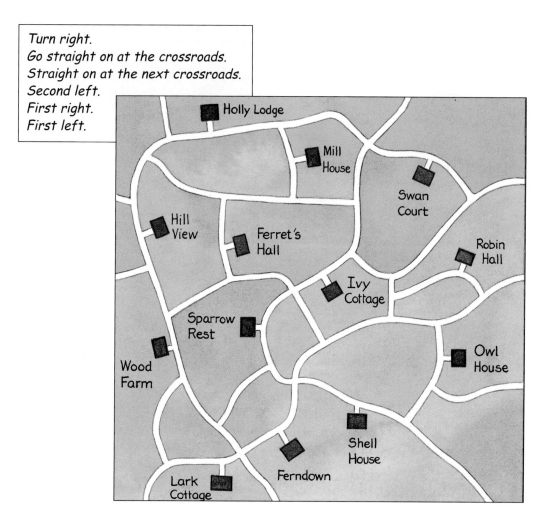

B6 Plan a journey on the map above.
Choose a starting point and write down directions for your journey.
Then give someone else your starting point and directions and see if they finish at the same place as you.

Challenge

Give your directions to someone else but tell them the **finishing** point and not the starting point.

See if they can work out where your journey started!

 **Gridlock**

This game is described in the teacher's guide.

Grid 1:
```
4  2  | 6 ✓
5  1  | 6 ✓
9  3    5
```
Points scored: 2

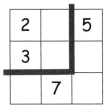

Grid 2:
```
3   2   6  | 11 ✓
2   5   5  | 12
6   3   2  | 11 ✓
11  10  13   10 ✓
  ✓     ✓
```
Points scored: 5

1 (a) Copy and complete these grids.
Find the points scored for each one.

```
2     | 5
3     |
   7
```
Points scored: ...

```
         | 5
      6  | 9
   7
```
Points scored: ...

```
         6  | 12
5           1  | 9
               6  | 16
      13       10
```
Points scored: ...

(b) Make up some problems like this for someone else to try.

2 Tom has made this grid
with 2, 3, 5 and 6.
He has scored 0 points.

Show how he could score
2 points with 2, 3, 5 and 6.

```
5   2  | 7
6   3  | 9
11  5    8
```
Points scored: 0

3 In one game, the numbers 6, 4, 3 and 6 were called.
One pupil scored 2 points and one scored 4 points.

With the numbers 6, 4, 3 and 6, show how you could score

(a) 2 points   (b) 4 points

4 With the numbers 1, 2, 3 and 4,

   (a) what is the highest number of points you can score

   (b) what is the lowest number of points you can score

5 Copy and complete these 'Gridlock' grids.

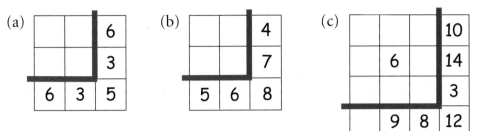

6 Find a set of four numbers that will always give
   you a score of 0 points.

7 Explain why you will always score 5 points with
   the numbers 1, 2, 2 and 2.

8 Explain why you will always score some points
   with the numbers 1, 1, 5 and 2.

9 Copy and complete these grids.

(a)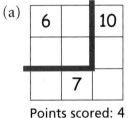

Points scored: 4

(b)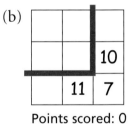

Points scored: 0

10 With the numbers 1, 2, 2, 3, 4, 5, 5, 6 and 6,
   show how you could score

   (a) 6 points   (b) 7 points   (c) 0 points

11 Copy and complete this grid with
   the numbers 1, 1, 3, 4, 5, 5, 5, 6 and 6.

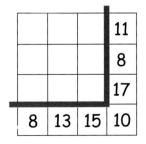

Year planner

You need sheet 50.

30 days hath September,
April, June and November,
All the rest have 31,
Excepting February alone,
Which has but 28 days clear,
And 29 in each leap year.

Write the dates in each month on the planner.
You can then use the planner to show holidays,
birthdays and so on.

Use this ↓

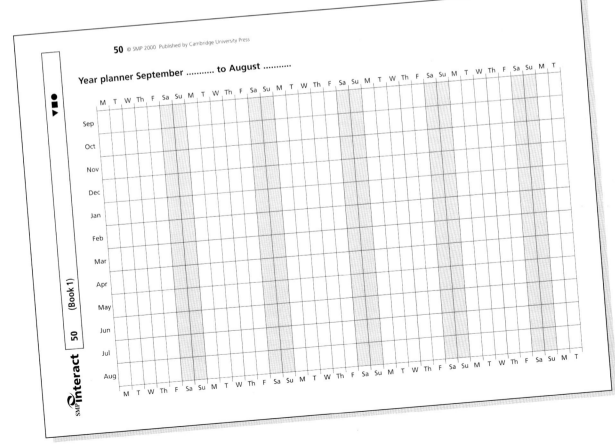

S8 Patterns from a hexagon

The patterns here are based on a regular hexagon.
Drawing the patterns will help you improve your drawing skills.

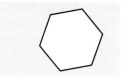

Practise drawing a regular hexagon like this.

1 Set a pair of compasses to about 4 cm apart.

Draw a circle.

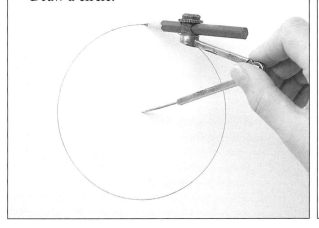

2 Do not change the compasses.
Put the point anywhere on the circle.

Make a mark like this.

3 Make another mark like this …

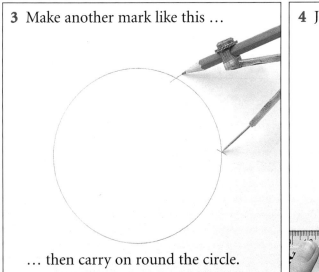

… then carry on round the circle.

4 Join the points to draw the hexagon.

These designs are based on a regular hexagon.
Use the compasses method to help you draw some of them.

Colour your drawings.
Choose your own colours.

Use compasses to make up designs of your own.

For some patterns you need to draw lines or circles
and then rub parts of them out.

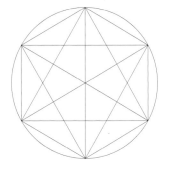

1 Draw a regular hexagon.
Join all the corners with
faint lines.

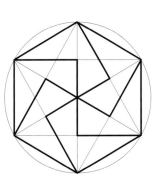

2 Go over these lines
more strongly.

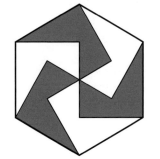

3 Rub out lines you don't
need.
Colour in the pattern.

Use the rub-out method to draw some of these.
Colour your drawings.

 **Tangrams**

Cut out a square from sheet 51.
Cut it into seven pieces, as shown here.

The pieces are called 'tans'.
They can be arranged, without
overlapping, to make shapes.

Pictures made with all seven tans are
called 'tangrams'.

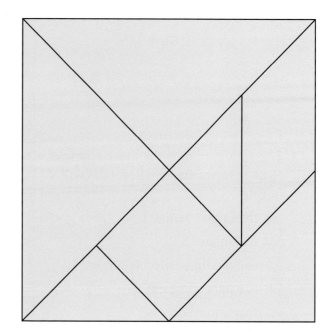

This is an example of a tangram.

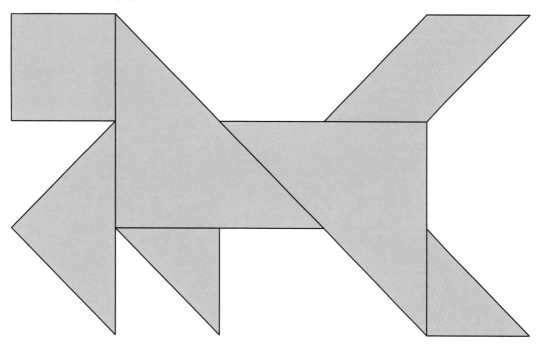

1 Make the shapes on sheet 52.
  Draw lines to show how the tans fit.

2 Make your own tangram with the seven tans.
  Draw its outline and give it to someone else to make.

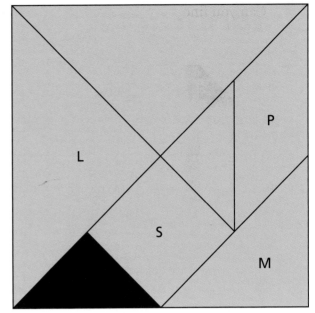

3 The smallest tan is the black triangle. How many of the smallest tans will fit into

   (a) the large triangle L

   (b) the square S

   (c) the medium-sized triangle M

   (d) the parallelogram P

   (e) the whole square

4 This boat shape can be made with 5 smallest tans. Its **area** is 5 smallest tans.

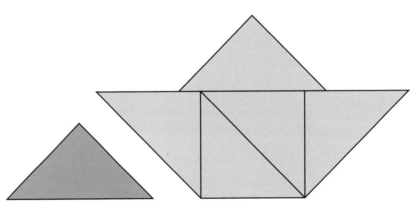

   Find the area, in smallest tans, of each shape on sheets 53 and 54.

5 You need sheet 55.

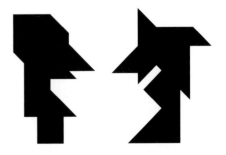

*6 Can you find the area, in smallest tans, of each of these holes?

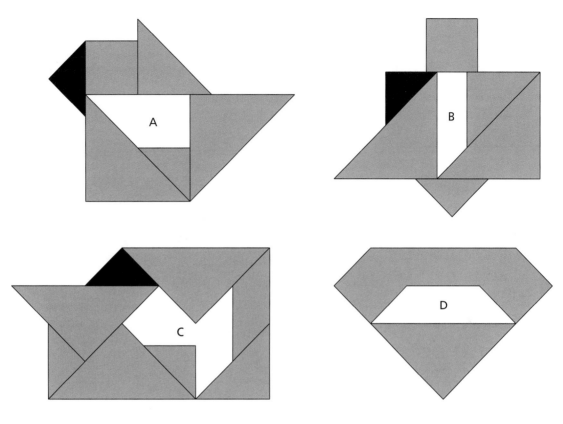

⑩ Half a square

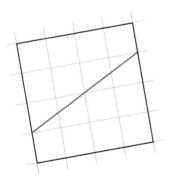
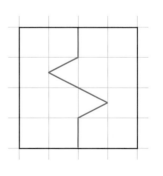
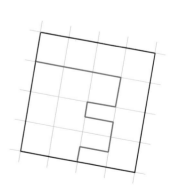

Use one of these ideas, or one of your own.

Split a square in half by

- drawing one straight line
- starting and finishing on opposite sides
- starting and finishing on adjacent sides

Pentominoes

A Finding pentominoes

A pentomino is made with five squares.

Squares are joined together
edge to edge like this.

These are not allowed.

- Find the pentominoes which are made by
  adding one more square onto this.

- Find all the other pentominoes.

- How can you be sure you have found them all?

- How can you be sure you have not found the
  same pentomino twice?

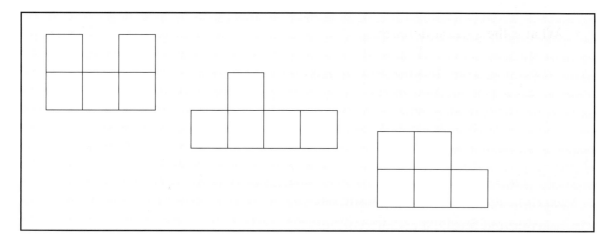

B The 8 by 8 game

This is a game for two or three players.

You need sheets 56 and 57.

- Cut out the set of pentominoes on sheet 56.

- Take turns to place a pentomino on the board (sheet 57).
  You must not overlap any pentomino already on the board.

- The winner is the last player to place a pentomino on the board.

- What is the smallest number of pentominoes
  that can be on the board at the end of a game?

- What is the greatest number?

C Pentomino fields

- Use a set of pentominoes to make a fence around a field.
  You must join pentominoes edge to edge correctly.

- Make the field as large as you can.

There are four levels of difficulty.

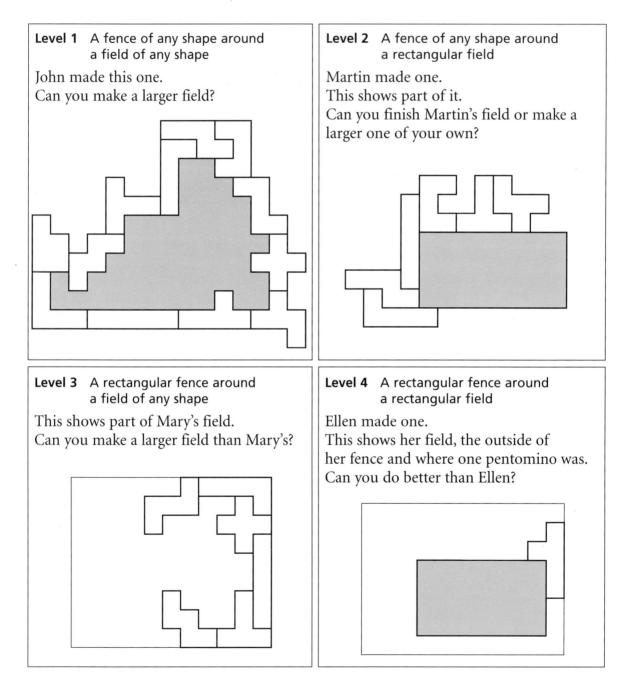

Level 1   A fence of any shape around
a field of any shape

John made this one.
Can you make a larger field?

Level 2   A fence of any shape around
a rectangular field

Martin made one.
This shows part of it.
Can you finish Martin's field or make a
larger one of your own?

Level 3   A rectangular fence around
a field of any shape

This shows part of Mary's field.
Can you make a larger field than Mary's?

Level 4   A rectangular fence around
a rectangular field

Ellen made one.
This shows her field, the outside of
her fence and where one pentomino was.
Can you do better than Ellen?

Shapes on a dotty square

Rules

- Every corner must be at one of the nine dots.

- These are not allowed:

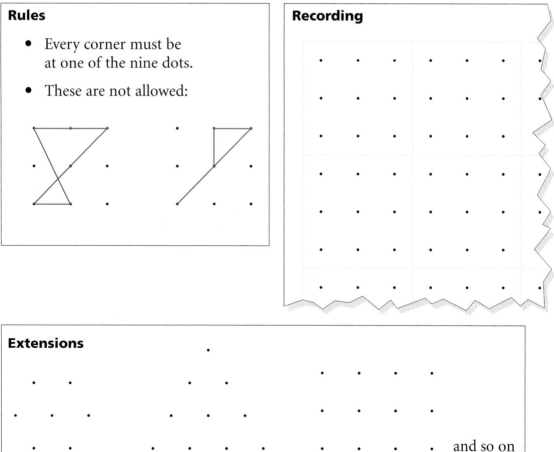

Recording

Extensions

and so on

❶ Reflection symmetry

This is about making shapes using mirrors and folding.
The work will help you

◆ make shapes that have reflection symmetry

◆ identify symmetrical shapes and their lines of symmetry

A Folding and cutting ▼■●

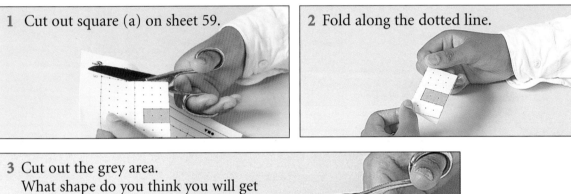

1 Cut out square (a) on sheet 59.

2 Fold along the dotted line.

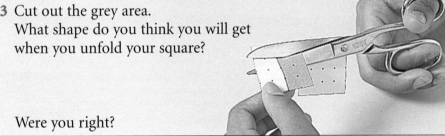

3 Cut out the grey area.
What shape do you think you will get
when you unfold your square?

Were you right?

A1 For each square (b) to (e) on sheet 59

• draw the shape you think you will get if you
fold along the dotted line and cut out the grey area

• try it and see if you were right

A2 On square (f)

• draw your own shape on one side of the dotted line

• ask someone else to draw the shape you will get if
you fold along the dotted line and cut out your shape

• cut out the shape to see if they are right

▼■○ **A3** Try the problems on sheet 60.

▼■● **A4** Try the problems on sheet 61.

▽■● **A5** Try the problems on sheet 62.

B Using a mirror ▼■●

You need sheet 63.

B1 Put your mirror on the dotted line on diagram (a).

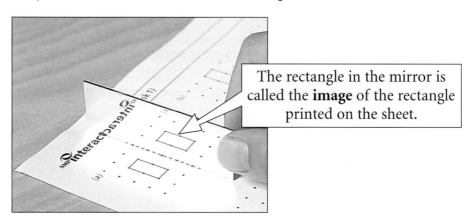

The rectangle in the mirror is called the **image** of the rectangle printed on the sheet.

Take the mirror away and
try to draw the image that you saw.

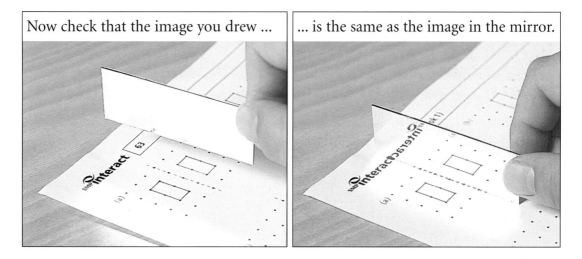

Now check that the image you drew ... ... is the same as the image in the mirror.

B2 Use a mirror to draw the images for diagrams (b) to (l).

After a while, you may be able to draw the image without using the mirror.
But always check with the mirror.

C Looking for reflection symmetry

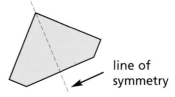

Shapes you can make with a mirror or by folding and cutting are called **symmetrical**.

The fold or the place where the mirror goes is called a **line of symmetry**.

line of symmetry

C1

> Put your mirror along the dotted line on shape (a) below.
> The shape you see is symmetrical, but …

> … it is not the rectangle printed on the page. So the dotted line is **not** a line of symmetry.

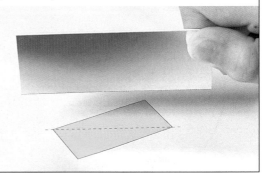

Is the dotted line a line of symmetry for each shape (b) to (h)?
Write 'yes' or 'no' for each one.
Check with your mirror.

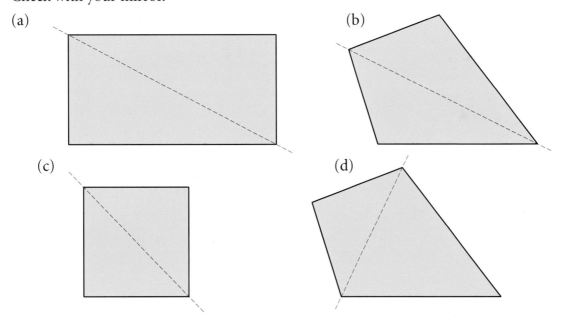

(a)

(b)

(c)

(d)

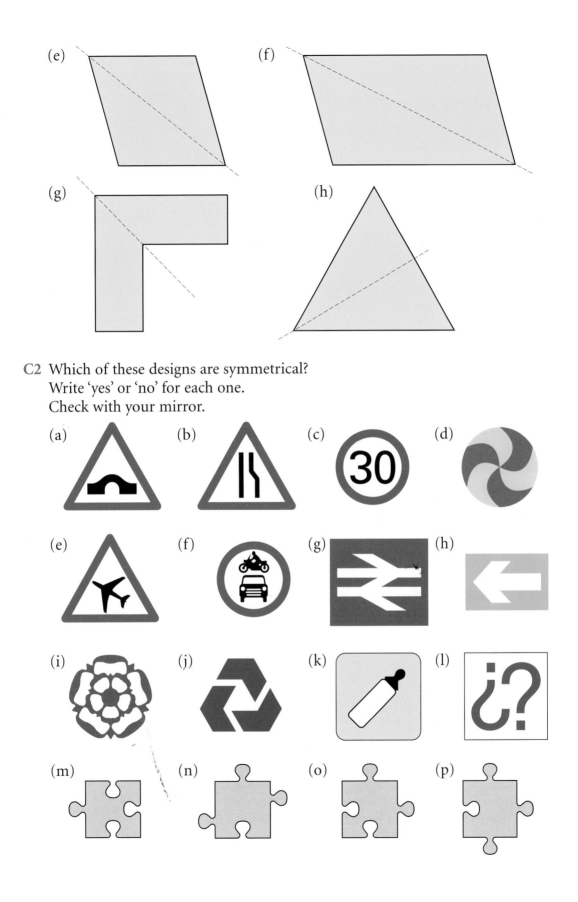

(e)

(f)

(g)

(h)

C2 Which of these designs are symmetrical?
Write 'yes' or 'no' for each one.
Check with your mirror.

(a)

(b)

(c)

(d)

(e)

(f)

(g)

(h)

(i)

(j)

(k)

(l)

(m)

(n)

(o)

(p)

D Times and dates ▼■●

Peter's computer shows the time on the screen.　**06:20**

The times are sometimes symmetrical, like this:　- - - **18:03** - - - .

D1 (a) Which of these times are symmetrical?

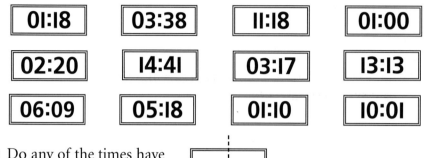

01:18	**03:38**	**11:18**	**01:00**
02:20	**14:41**	**03:17**	**13:13**
06:09	**05:18**	**01:10**	**10:01**

　(b) Do any of the times have two lines of symmetry?

　(c) Write three more times that have one line of symmetry.

　(d) Write one more time that has two lines of symmetry.

Peter's computer shows the date in a similar way.

D2 11 November 2011 looks like this.　**11:11:11**

How many lines of symmetry does it have?

D3 3 August 2001 looks like this.　**03:08:01**

Is this date symmetrical?

D4 Say whether each of these dates has one, two or no lines of symmetry.

　(a) **06:01:08**　　　(b) **18:11:81**

　(c) **16:11:91**　　　(d) **08:10:13**

D5 Write these dates the way the computer shows them, and say how many lines of symmetry each one has.

　(a) 4 February 2033　　(b) 31 October 2081

　(c) 8 November 2080　　(d) 8 January 2080

D6 Write two more dates that have only one line of symmetry.

D7 Write two more dates that have two lines of symmetry.

You need the 25 tiles cut from sheet 64.

A design with one or more lines of symmetry has **reflection symmetry**.

E1 Pick out these four tiles.

Arrange them to make a pattern with reflection symmetry.
Make some more symmetrical patterns with them.

E2 Pick out these four tiles.

Make different symmetrical patterns with them.

E3 Pick out these two tiles

and arrange them like this.

Put a mirror along the dotted line
to make a symmetrical pattern.

E4 (a) Use a mirror and these two tiles

to make this pattern.

(b) Use a mirror and these two tiles

to make this.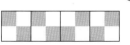

(c) Use a mirror and these two tiles

to make this.

31

E5 Pick out these three tiles

and arrange them like this.

Put a mirror along the dotted line
to make a symmetrical pattern.

E6 (a) Use a mirror and these three tiles

to make this.

(b) Use a mirror and these three tiles

to make this.

E7 Make each of these with two or three tiles and a mirror.
Draw a sketch of your tiles. Draw a dotted line to show where the mirror went.

E8 Try to find more than one way to make each of these with tiles and a mirror.

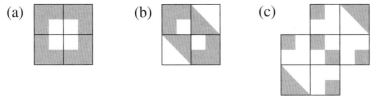

Keep all the tiles for the game.

Symmetry tiles game

for 2, 3 or 4 players

What you need

- You need a set of 25 tiles cut from sheet 64. There are five designs.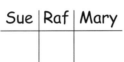

  Check that you have five tiles of each design.

- You also need a copy of board 1 on sheet 64.

The aim of the game

- You have to fill the board with a pattern that has a line of symmetry along the dotted line.

Before you start

- Make a score table like this with your own names.

Sue	Raf	Mary

- Deal out the tiles so each player has the same number. If there is a spare tile, don't use it.

When it is your turn

- Put one of your tiles on a square on the board. Remember that the pattern on the board must be symmetrical when the game is finished.

- Your score is the number you have covered up. Write your score in the score table.

- If you can't go you miss your turn.

The winner

- The winner is the player with most points at the end of the game.

You can use the same rules to play the game on boards 2 and 3 on sheet 65. These games are harder.

F Folding again ▽■●

F1 (a) Sarah has drawn this shape on 'twice-folded paper'.

Which of the shapes below will she get when she cuts it and opens it out?

P	Q	R	S

(b) Which of the shapes below will she get when she cuts this shape and opens it out?

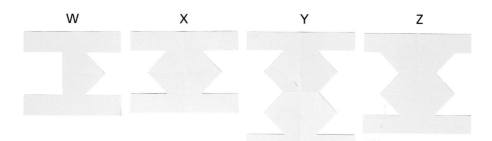

W	X	Y	Z

(c) Check your answers to (a) and (b) by drawing the shapes and cutting them out yourself.

F2 Which of these make letters of the alphabet when they are cut and opened out?

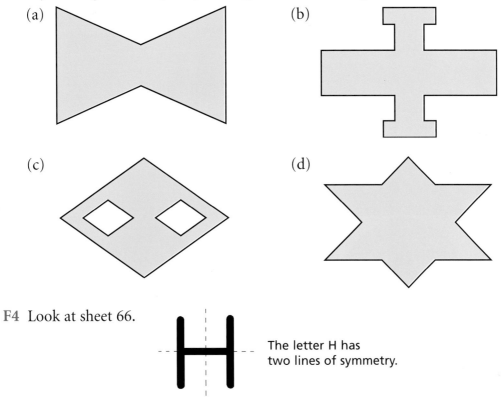

A   B   C   D

F3 Try making these shapes by folding twice and cutting.

(a)

(b)

(c)

(d)

F4 Look at sheet 66.

The letter H has two lines of symmetry.

(a) Which is the first letter with no line of symmetry?

(b) Draw any lines of symmetry on each letter.

(c) Copy this table. Write all the letters in it.

Number of lines of reflection symmetry	Letters
0	
1	A
2	
3	
4	
more than 4	

The letter A has been put in for you.

35

G Rangoli patterns

You need squared paper.

Rangoli patterns are used to decorate the homes
of Hindu and Sikh families.
They are often made for weddings and festivals
like Divali.
The patterns are sometimes made at the entrance to
their home.
Flower petals, rice and other seeds are used to colour
the designs.

G1 These rangoli patterns are symmetrical.
How many lines of symmetry does
each pattern have?

(a)

(b)

This is one way of drawing the outline of a rangoli pattern with four lines of symmetry.

Draw four lines of symmetry on squared paper.

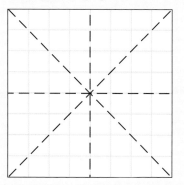

Draw some lines in one of the triangles.

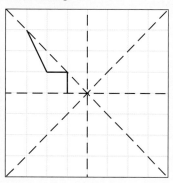

Reflect your lines in one of the sloping lines of symmetry.

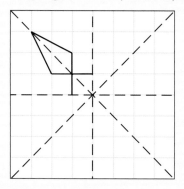

Reflect all your lines in the other sloping line of symmetry.

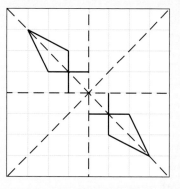

Reflect all your lines in the vertical line of symmetry.

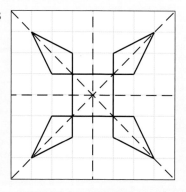

G2 Use this method to draw some rangoli patterns of your own.

H Shading squares

H1 How many different ways can you shade
three squares in this design so that
it has reflection symmetry?
Sketch your different ways.

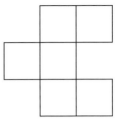

H2 Sketch all the different ways of shading
three squares in this design so that
it has reflection symmetry.

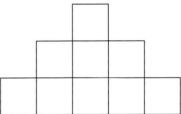

▽■● H3 Sketch all the different ways of shading
three squares in this design so that
it has reflection symmetry.

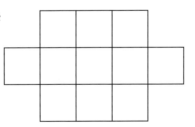

▽■● H4 How many different ways can you shade
two squares in this design so that
it has two lines of symmetry?
Sketch the different ways.

▽□● H5 How many different ways can you shade
four squares in this design so that it has
two (**but no more than two**) lines of symmetry?
Sketch the different ways.

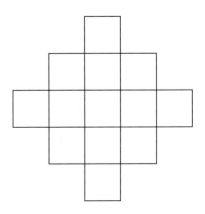

I Designs

I1 Look at the dotted lines on these designs.
Some of them are lines of symmetry.
Some of them are not lines of symmetry.

Which of the lines are lines of symmetry?
Decide without using a mirror.

Check with a mirror if you need to.

(a)

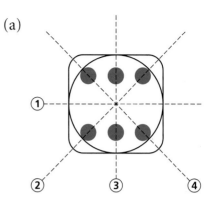

(b)

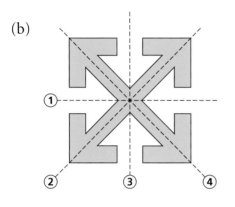

(c)

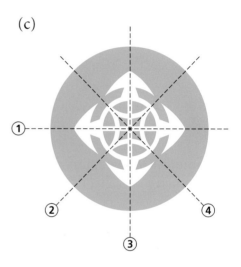

(d)

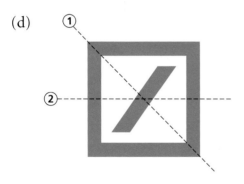

(e)

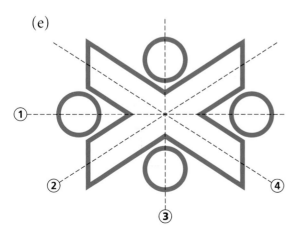

(f)

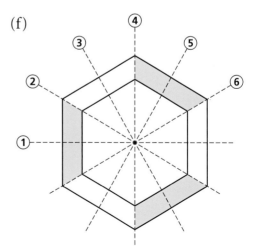

39

What progress have you made?

Statement

▼■●   I can complete a symmetrical
↓   shape when I have half of it.

Evidence

1   Copy and complete these symmetrical
    shapes.

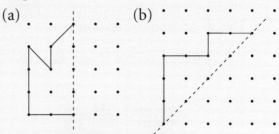

(a)   (b)

I can draw a line of symmetry
on a symmetrical shape.

2   Copy this shape and draw
    its line of symmetry.

▽■●   I can find all the lines of
symmetry of a shape.

3   Copy this design.
    Show all its lines
    of symmetry.

4   Which of these are
    lines of symmetry?

① ② ③ ④ ⑤ ⑥

▽□●   I can solve problems about
symmetry.

5   Sketch all the different
    ways you can shade
    four squares in this
    design so that it has
    four lines of symmetry.

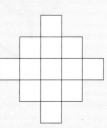

2 Test it!

This is about making and testing general statements
about body measurements.
The work will help you

◆ measure accurately

◆ collect and record data

A I don't believe it!

▼■●

Look at this statement.

'Everyone is
six and a half feet tall.'

Discuss these questions.

- *What does the statement mean?*

- *How could it be tested?*

- *What equipment will you need to test it?*

Draw up a plan together of how to test the statement.

Now put your plan into action.
Use it to answer the questions below.
(Don't be afraid to alter the plan as you go along.
Just make a note of any changes.)

- *Is the statement true for you?*

- *How true is it for your group?*

- *What about the rest of your class?*

B Organising your results

For class or group discussion

Amy, Ben, Emma and Anil have been set
the task of testing this statement:

> People's heights are three times
> the distance round their heads.

They measure each other's height
and head size.

They write the measurements down.

Anil 1.63 54

Emma 56/170

Amy 52 and 156

Ben 57,172

B1 Look carefully at their measurements.
Can you make sense of them?
Would they mean anything to a stranger?
How would you improve their method of recording results?

Amy writes all their results in a table.

This helps them see any connections
between height and head size.

Name	Head size (cm)	Height (cm)
Amy Allen	52	156
Anil Patel	54	163
Ben Arnot	57	172
Emma Pollock	56	170

B2 Ben says that their measurements show that

*'People's heights are approximately
three times the distance round their heads.'*

Is Ben's conclusion correct?

B3 A group of children measured themselves.
Here is their record of their data.

Name	Height (metres)	Distance round head (cm)	Arm span (cm)	Foot length (cm)	Head length (cm)	Hand span (cm)
Anna	1.41	53.5	152	19	21	16
Tim	1.63	57	1.70	29	23	20
Gina	14.4	54	143	21	21.5	19
Ajaz	1.49	55	153	22	23	19
Sue	159	59	157	2.6	23.5	21
Neena	1.48	54		23	23	19
Ryan	0.15	53	154	25	20.5	18
Lara	1.36	52	133	18	20.5	7
Majid	1.5	54	148	24	23.5	18

(a) What do you think 'head length' means?
How would you measure it?

(b) Some children made mistakes.
Find the mistakes and suggest what the measurements might be.

(c) To go on some fairground rides, you have to be at least 1.5 m tall.
Who can go on these rides?

(d) Neena's arm span was not measured.
Can you suggest what it might have been?

(e) In this group, whose height is closest to your height?
Whose foot length is closest to your foot length?
Whose arm span is closest to your arm span?

(f) Roughly how many times does head length go into height?

C Now it's your turn!

For two or more people

Here is a collection of statements about body size.

- The height of a person is equal to their arm span.
- People's waists are roughly twice the distance round their necks.
- A person's head length is half the distance across their shoulders.
- The distance round people's fists is the same as their foot length.

Choose one of the statements about body size.
Discuss how you would test it.
This checklist may help you.

> - *How many people will we measure?*
> - *What equipment will we need?*
> - *How will we record the data?*
> - *How can our group check the measuring and recording?*

Carry out your plan.
Do your results agree with the statement?

D Number detective

▽□●

You need a calculator for this section.

D1 Six people's heights (in cm) and the distances from
their elbow to finger tips (in cm) were measured.
The results are shown in this table.

(a) Look at the first pair of results.
How many times does the distance
from elbow to finger tip
go into the height?

(b) Copy the table and fill in the
third column.

(c) Look at all the figures in the
third column of your table.
Is there an approximate connection
between height and elbow distance?

Height (cm)	Distance from elbow to finger tip (cm)	Height ÷ distance
160	40	
136.5	35	
175.5	45	
161	41	
133	35	
152	42	

Amazing but true!

There is a rough rule connecting the distance round an elephant's foot print and its height. It is

Use the data in the table below to help you find what this rough rule might be.

Elephant's name	Height (cm)	Distance round foot (cm)
Ela	96	50
Anita	120	64
Ravi	150	80
Tarak	200	105
Sikta	280	150
Aslam	330	170

D3 See if you can find a relationship between any pair of these body measurements.

height
length of middle finger
hand span
height to top of knee
foot length
width of hand
arm span
length of ear

What progress have you made?

Statement

▼■● I can collect and record information, and can test statements.

▽□● I can find approximate rules between measurements.

Evidence

Your work in sections A and C will show this.

1 Find an approximate rule connecting these pairs of measurements.

Height (cm)	Hand length (cm)
185	20
150	16
163	18
156	17
172	19

③ Coordinates

This is about archaeological digs.
The work will help you use coordinates.

A Recording positions ▼■●

A farmer walked across his field one day.
He saw something shine in the ground.
He picked it up. It was a gold Roman coin
nearly 2000 years old.

The farmer wrote a letter to the local college.
He said a team of experts could dig up the
field.

Dr Sanders came with a team of diggers.
She made careful notes every time a digger
found something.

She noted the exact place where each object
was found.

The map opposite shows what the diggers found in the first month.
They found some walls and a few objects.

Look where the gold coins were found.

The **coordinates** of this point are **(1, 4)**.

metres **across** the field   metres **up** the field

A1 What was found at (a) (4, 1) (b) (8, 5) (c) (5, 8)

A2 Where did the diggers find these?

  (a) Broken pot   (b) Bones   (c) Bronze coins

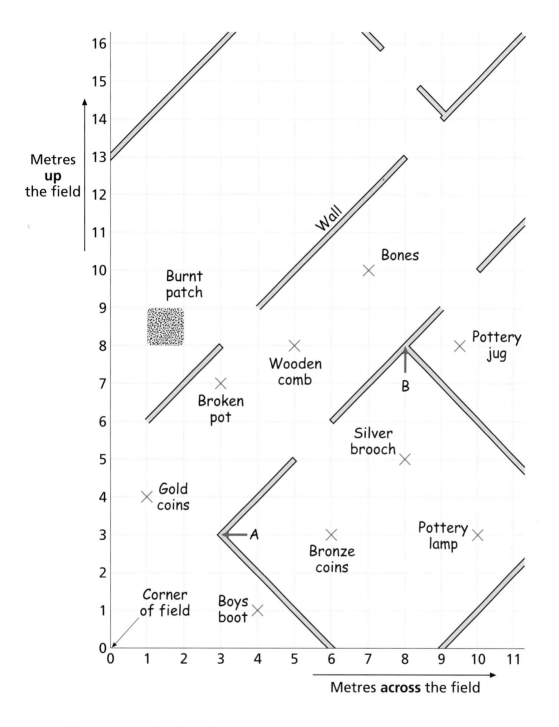

A3 What starts at (4, 9) and goes to (8, 13)?

A4 Find the corner of the field on the map. What are its coordinates?

A5 The corners of a room are labelled A and B.
What are their coordinates?

A6 You need sheet 67.

Here are Dr Sanders's notes for the second month.
Mark each object on the map and write its name.

Bones at (8, 14)

Broken pots at (2, 18) and (3, 15)

Grave between (2, 21) and (4, 20)

Arrowheads at (11, 15)

Wall from (5, 10) to (1, 14)

Parade helmet (8, 19)

Round grain pit 2 metres across
centre at (4, 23)

Gold ring (15, 20)

Body scraper (13, 12)

Wall from (1, 6) to (0, 7)

Human skull (11, 23)

B Digging deeper

After one year the diggers decided to dig deeper.
They found the remains of buildings in layers.
The buildings got older as they dug deeper.

Level 1
(Last Roman)

Level 2
(Roman)

Level 3
(First Roman)

Level 4
(Iron Age)

There were four levels of old buildings.
Dr Sanders made a different map for each level.
The map you have used already is level 1.
The other levels are on sheets 68 and 69.

▼□○ **B1** You need sheet 68 (level 2).
Mark each of these objects on the map of level 2.

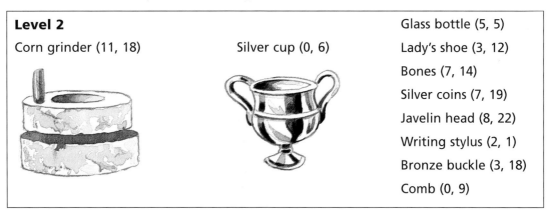

Level 2

Corn grinder (11, 18)   Silver cup (0, 6)

Glass bottle (5, 5)

Lady's shoe (3, 12)

Bones (7, 14)

Silver coins (7, 19)

Javelin head (8, 22)

Writing stylus (2, 1)

Bronze buckle (3, 18)

Comb (0, 9)

▽■● **B2** You need sheet 69 (levels 3 and 4).
Mark each of these finds on the level 3 map.

Level 3

Gold bracelet
$(1\frac{1}{2}, 14\frac{1}{2})$

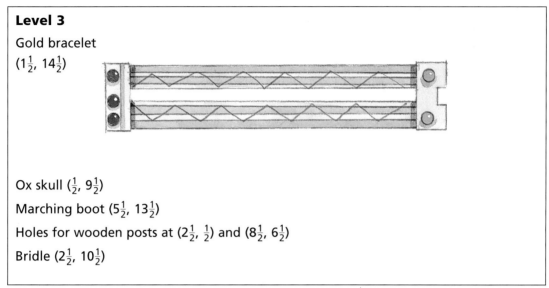

Ox skull $(\frac{1}{2}, 9\frac{1}{2})$

Marching boot $(5\frac{1}{2}, 13\frac{1}{2})$

Holes for wooden posts at $(2\frac{1}{2}, \frac{1}{2})$ and $(8\frac{1}{2}, 6\frac{1}{2})$

Bridle $(2\frac{1}{2}, 10\frac{1}{2})$

▽■● **B3** Mark each of these finds on the level 4 map.

Level 4

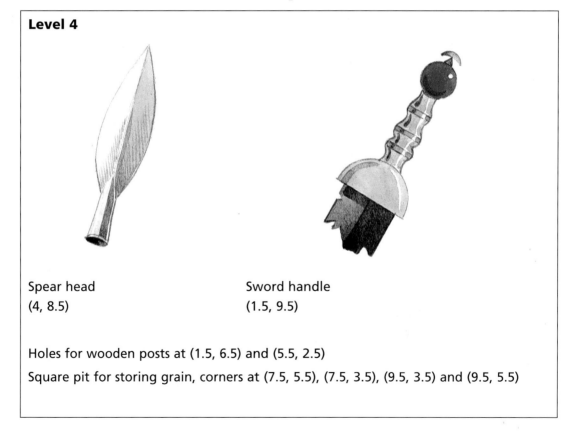

Spear head
(4, 8.5)

Sword handle
(1.5, 9.5)

Holes for wooden posts at (1.5, 6.5) and (5.5, 2.5)

Square pit for storing grain, corners at (7.5, 5.5), (7.5, 3.5), (9.5, 3.5) and (9.5, 5.5)

C Negative coordinates

Diggers working on level 1 sometimes found an object outside the field.

They needed to use **negative numbers** for the coordinates.

The coordinates of the silver coin are

(⁻5, 3)

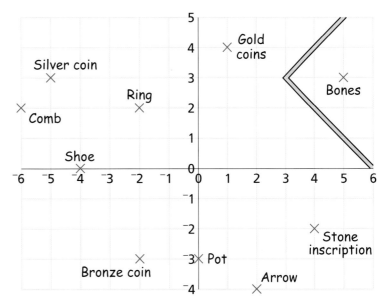

C1 Write down the coordinates of
- (a) the ring
- (b) the stone inscription
- (c) the bronze coin
- (d) the arrow
- (e) the shoe
- (f) the comb
- (g) the pot

C2 Copy this grid and mark each object on it.

Silver ring (⁻1, 4)

Coin (5, ⁻1)

Buckle (⁻3, 0)

Dagger (⁻5, ⁻4)

Cup (0, ⁻5)

Line of wall
from (⁻5, 1) to (3, 5)
and from (3, 5) to (6, ⁻1)
and from (6, ⁻1) to (0, ⁻4)

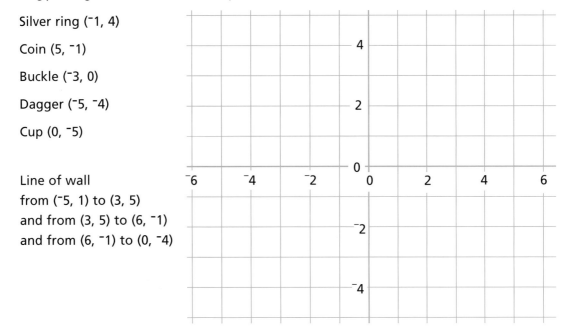

C3 This broken floor pattern was found on another dig.

When it was complete, it consisted of a four-pointed star inside a square.

(a) What are the coordinates of the three missing corners of the square?

(b) What are the coordinates of the two missing points of the star?

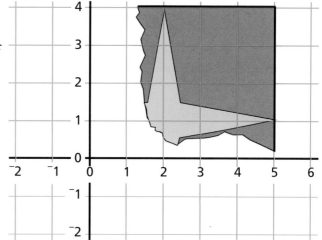

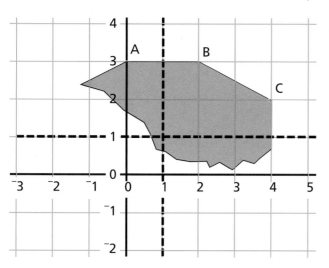

C4 This broken floor was originally an eight-sided shape.

The dotted lines show where the lines of symmetry were.

Only three of the corners of the shape remain (A, B and C).

What were the coordinates of the other five corners?

C5 This map comes from another dig. It shows the foundations of a building with four rectangular rooms.

(a) Work out, without drawing, the coordinates of the fourth corner of each room.

(b) Work out the coordinates of the point at the centre of each room.

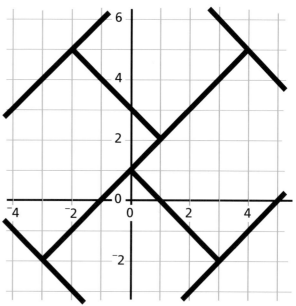

*C6

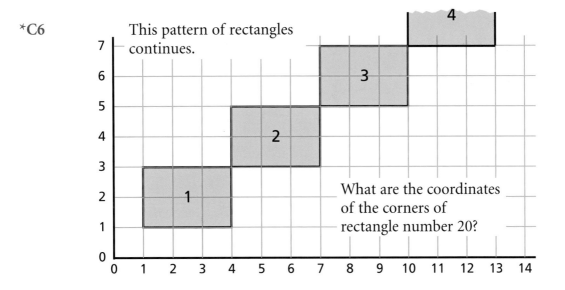

This pattern of rectangles continues.

What are the coordinates of the corners of rectangle number 20?

What progress have you made?

Statement

Evidence

▼■● I can write the coordinates of a
↓   point.

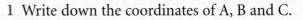

1 Write down the coordinates of A, B and C.

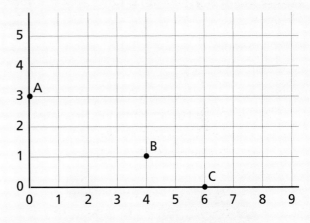

I can plot points on a grid.

2 Copy the grid above and mark the points D (3, 4) and E (0, 2).

▽□● I understand negative coordinates.

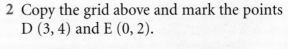

3 Plot the points (⁻7, 2), (⁻3, ⁻6) and (1, ⁻2) on a grid of your own.

④ Oral questions 1

This work will help you
- ◆ find information from a table
- ◆ answer spoken questions

diameter

Tenpin bowling

Here is some information about the balls used in different sports.

Game	Diameter (cm)	Weight (g)	Cost (£)
Bowls (bowl)	11.7–13.3	1590	£100 for 4
Bowls (jack)	6.3–6.4	227–283	£12
Cricket	7.1–7.3	155–163	£7.50
Football	21.8–22.6	396–453	£7.50–£30
Golf	4.3	45.9	£1.30
Netball	21	400–450	£9
Pool	5.7	156–170	£30 (set of 15)
Rounders	5.4–6.0	70–85	£4
Shot (men)	11–13	7260	£10
Shot (women)	9.5–11	4000	£10
Table tennis	3.8	2.5	£3.00 for 6
Tenpin bowling	21.6	7258	£80 for a pair
Tennis	6.8	56.7–58.5	£3.90 for 3

Cricket

Golf

Tennis

Netball

Pool

Bowls

Shot put

Table tennis

Rounders

Football

Brackets

This is about using brackets in expressions.
The work will help you

- ◆ use brackets to show which part of a calculation is done first
- ◆ work out the value of expressions that use brackets

A Check it out

Mrs Turner's class were given some homework to do.
They had to make some **expressions** that gave 24.
Here are some of their homeworks.

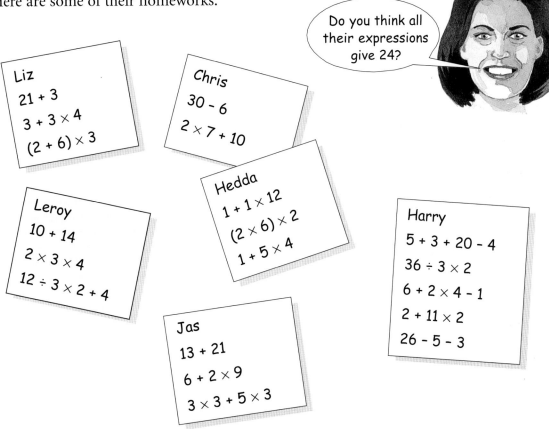

Do you think all their expressions give 24?

Liz
21 + 3
3 + 3 × 4
(2 + 6) × 3

Chris
30 – 6
2 × 7 + 10

Leroy
10 + 14
2 × 3 × 4
12 ÷ 3 × 2 + 4

Hedda
1 + 1 × 12
(2 × 6) × 2
1 + 5 × 4

Harry
5 + 3 + 20 – 4
36 ÷ 3 × 2
6 + 2 × 4 – 1
2 + 11 × 2
26 – 5 – 3

Jas
13 + 21
6 + 2 × 9
3 × 3 + 5 × 3

- ● You could make your own list of expressions that give 24.
  Ask a friend to check them.

A1 Work these out without using a calculator.

(a) $(3 + 1) \times 2$

(b) $5 + (2 \times 4)$

(c) $(8 - 3) \times 2$

(d) $8 + (3 \times 5)$

(e) $16 + (8 \div 2)$

(f) $(20 - 10) \div 5$

(g) $15 + (15 \div 3)$

(h) $(2 \times 3) - 6$

(i) $(5 - 2) \times (3 + 1)$

(j) $(12 - 6) \div 2$

(k) $12 - (6 \div 2)$

(l) $18 - (5 \times 3)$

A2 Copy these calculations. Use brackets to show which part of the calculation is done first.

(a) $6 - 1 \times 3 = 15$

(b) $4 \times 1 + 2 = 12$

(c) $2 + 1 \times 5 = 15$

(d) $6 \div 3 + 9 = 11$

(e) $2 + 3 \times 4 = 14$

(f) $5 \times 2 - 1 = 5$

(g) $5 - 1 \times 4 = 16$

(h) $2 + 2 \times 2 = 6$

(i) $3 \times 3 - 3 = 0$

(j) $4 + 4 \div 4 = 2$

(k) $12 \div 3 \times 2 = 2$

(l) $10 - 6 - 2 = 6$

A3 Sort these into three matching pairs.

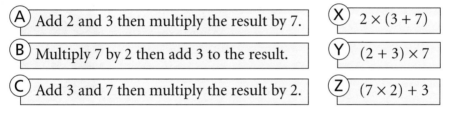

(A) Add 2 and 3 then multiply the result by 7.

(B) Multiply 7 by 2 then add 3 to the result.

(C) Add 3 and 7 then multiply the result by 2.

(X) $2 \times (3 + 7)$

(Y) $(2 + 3) \times 7$

(Z) $(7 \times 2) + 3$

A4 Find the missing numbers to make these calculations correct.

(a) $(1 + \square) \times 2 = 10$

(b) $(\square - 2) \times 4 = 12$

(c) $(3 \times \square) - 5 = 4$

(d) $2 \times (10 - \square) = 4$

(e) $4 \times (\square - 3) = 40$

(f) $(6 + \square) \div 3 = 5$

(g) $9 \div (\square + 4) = 1$

(h) $10 \div (6 - \square) = 2$

(i) $20 \div (\square + 6) = 2$

(j) $(4 \times 3) - (5 - \square) = 9$

A5 How many different numbers can you find using
2, 3, 5, +, × and one set of brackets?
Use 2, 3, 5, + and × exactly once in each calculation.

For example   *(5 + 2) × 3 = 21*

A6 Make up as many expressions as you can which have a value of 4.
In each expression use the digits 2, 4 and 6 once only.
You can use any of +, −, ×, ÷ and brackets as often as you like.

B Three in a row

A game for two or more players

What you need

- You need three dice.
  You also need to make a copy of the game board shown below.

When it is your turn

- Roll the three dice.

- Use the numbers and brackets to make an expression
  that has a value on the board.

- Write down your calculation for the other players to check.
  They can challenge you and get a free go if
  your calculation is incorrect or hasn't got any brackets.

- If you are correct you cross out the value of the
  expression on the board (or cover it with a counter).

7	8	9	10
6	1	2	11
5	4	3	12
16	15	14	13

The winner

- The winner is the first player to cross out three numbers in a row
  (across, down or diagonally).

C Brackets galore!

C1 Expressions may have more than one set of brackets.
Without using a calculator, work out the value of these expressions.

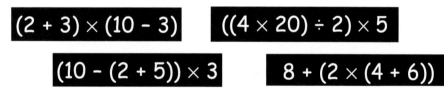

$$(2 + 3) \times (10 - 3) \qquad ((4 \times 20) \div 2) \times 5$$

$$(10 - (2 + 5)) \times 3 \qquad 8 + (2 \times (4 + 6))$$

C2 You can use brackets to give different values
for the expression $5 + 3 \times 4 - 1$.

For example, $((5 + 3) \times 4) - 1 = 31$.

Find as many different values as you can for

(a) $5 + 3 \times 4 - 1$ (b) $12 \div 2 + 4 \times 2$

▽□● C3 What different values can you find for $9 \times 4 \div 2 \times 3 - 1$?

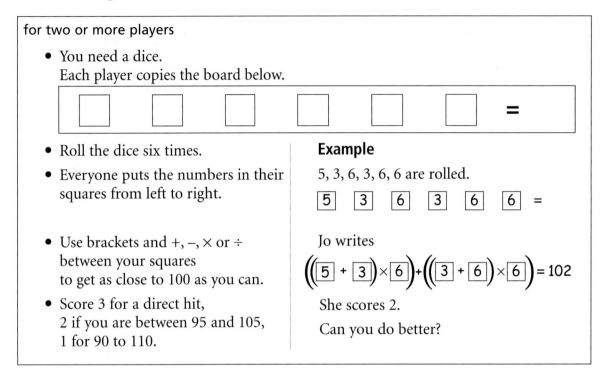

for two or more players

- You need a dice.
  Each player copies the board below.

- Roll the dice six times.
- Everyone puts the numbers in their squares from left to right.

- Use brackets and +, −, × or ÷ between your squares to get as close to 100 as you can.
- Score 3 for a direct hit, 2 if you are between 95 and 105, 1 for 90 to 110.

Example

5, 3, 6, 3, 6, 6 are rolled.

5 3 6 3 6 6 =

Jo writes

$$((5 + 3) \times 6) + ((3 + 6) \times 6) = 102$$

She scores 2.

Can you do better?

What progress have you made?

Statement	Evidence
▼■● ↓ I can work out expressions that use brackets.	1 Work these out. (a) $(7 \times 2) + 1$ (b) $(1 + 4) \times 2$ (c) $(20 + 10) \div 3$ (d) $5 \times (7 - 3)$ (e) $8 \div (1 + 3)$ (f) $(1 \times 2) + (3 \times 4)$
I can use brackets in expressions.	2 Copy these calculations and use brackets to show which part of the calculation is done first. (a) $6 + 1 \times 2 = 14$ (b) $3 \times 10 - 8 = 6$ (c) $10 - 6 \div 2 = 7$
▽■● I can use more than one set of brackets.	Your work in section C gives evidence of this.

⑥ Oral questions 2

This work will help you

◆ choose the information you need to solve a problem

◆ answer spoken questions

Here is a page from a stationery catalogue.

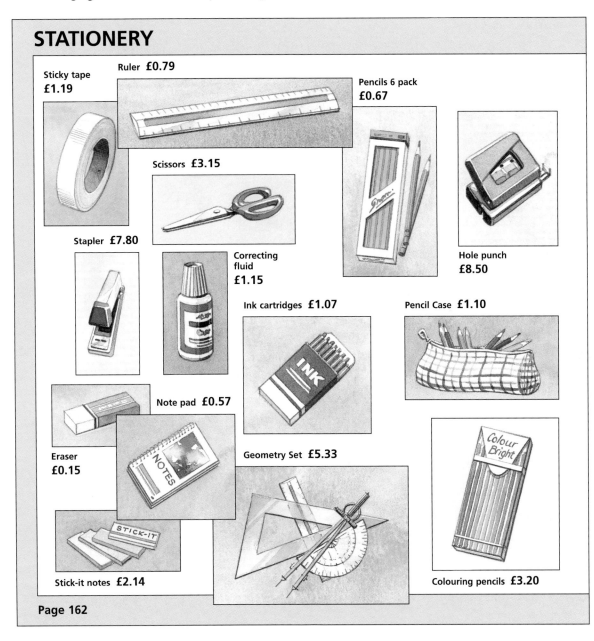

STATIONERY

Sticky tape **£1.19**

Ruler **£0.79**

Pencils 6 pack **£0.67**

Scissors **£3.15**

Stapler **£7.80**

Correcting fluid **£1.15**

Hole punch **£8.50**

Ink cartridges **£1.07**

Pencil Case **£1.10**

Note pad **£0.57**

Eraser **£0.15**

Geometry Set **£5.33**

Stick-it notes **£2.14**

Colouring pencils **£3.20**

Page 162

Review 1

▽□● 1 Copy these shapes and draw
↓   their lines of symmetry.

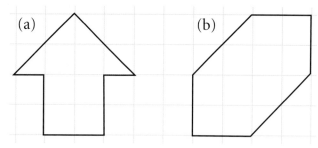

(a)   (b)

2 Work these out.

   (a) $5 + (3 \times 4)$ (b) $13 - (4 - 1)$ (c) $(3 + 4) \times 2$ (d) $24 - (8 \div 2)$

3 Write down the coordinates of the
   points A, B, C and D.

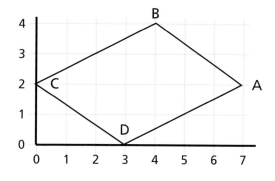

4 Copy these calculations and use brackets to show
   which part is done first.

   (a) $2 \times 5 + 3 = 16$ (b) $20 - 10 \div 2 = 5$ (c) $20 - 10 \div 2 = 15$

5 Which of the dotted lines are lines of symmetry?

   (a)   **2**   **3**   **4**   (b)

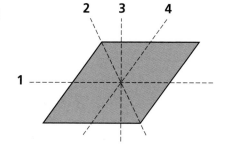 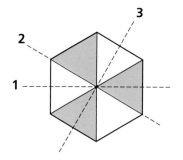

6 Work out the missing numbers.

   (a) $(5 + \square) \div 2 = 4$ (b) $12 - (\square + 1) = 3$ (c) $6 \times (\square - 1) = 30$

7 The points P, Q and R are three corners of a square.

(a) What are the coordinates of the fourth corner of the square?

(b) What are the coordinates of the point halfway between P and Q?

(c) What are the coordinates of the point halfway between Q and R?

(d) What are the coordinates of the point which is at the centre of the square?

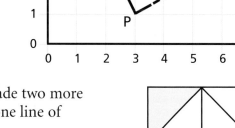

▽□● 8 (a) Sketch all the different ways you can shade two more triangles to make this design have just one line of symmetry.

(b) Sketch all the different ways you can shade any number of extra triangles to make the design have just two lines of symmetry.

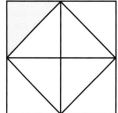

9 (a) Write down the coordinates of C.

(b) A, B and C are three of the corners of a square.
Without drawing, work out the coordinates of the fourth corner.

(c) P and Q are two of the corners of another square.
Work out the coordinates of the other two corners.

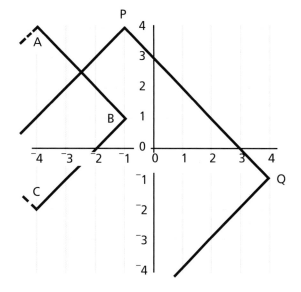

10 What different results can you get from arranging these cards to make a calculation?

For example, you can get $8 + (4 \div 2) = 10$, or $4 \div (8 + 2) = 0.4, \ldots$

⑦ Growing patterns

This is about investigating patterns.
The work will help you

◆ find patterns in a variety of situations

◆ describe how a pattern continues

◆ explain why a pattern continues in a particular way

A Coming up roses   ▼■●

This activity is described in the teacher's guide.

B Pond life   ▼■●

Joe works in a garden centre that sells square ponds
and square slabs to go round them.
Each slab measures 1 metre by 1 metre.

Joe works out how many slabs are needed for each pond.

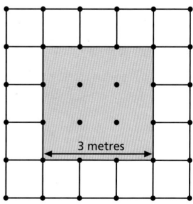

B1 Here are his diagrams for the first three ponds:

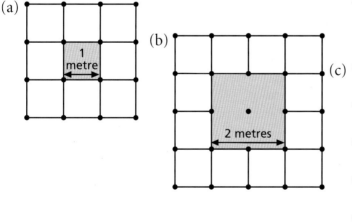

How many slabs are needed for each pond?

B2 (a) Draw a diagram for a pond that measures 4 by 4 metres.

(b) How many slabs are needed for this pond?

B3 (a) Draw a diagram for a pond that measures 5 by 5 metres.

(b) How many slabs are needed for this pond?

B4 (a) Copy and complete the table.

Side length of pond	1 metre	2 metres	3 metres	4 metres	5 metres	6 metres
Number of slabs						

(b) How many slabs do you think will be needed for a pond that measures 7 by 7 metres?

(c) Check your result by drawing.

(d) How many slabs will be needed for a pond that measures 10 by 10 metres? Show how you worked this out.

B5 What size of pond needs 48 slabs to go round it? Show how you worked this out.

B6 (a) Describe how the number of slabs needed goes up as the size of the pond goes up.

(b) Explain why the number of slabs goes up in this way.

B7 A 67 by 67 metre pond needs 272 slabs. How many slabs are needed for a pond that measures 68 by 68 metres?

▽■● **B8** How many slabs would be needed for a pond that measures 15 by 15 metres? Show how you worked out your answer.

▽□● **B9** Which of these gives how many slabs are needed for a square pond that measures n by n metres?

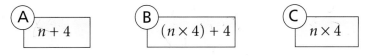

A $n + 4$ B $(n \times 4) + 4$ C $n \times 4$

C Changing shape

C1 The garden centre also sells rectangular ponds.
All the rectangular ponds are 3 metres wide.

(a) How many slabs are needed for these ponds?

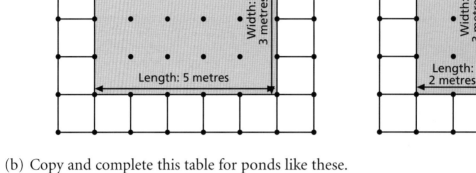

(b) Copy and complete this table for ponds like these.

3 metre wide ponds							
Length of pond	1 metre	2 metres	3 metres	4 metres	5 metres	6 metres	7 metres
Number of slabs							

(c) How many slabs do you think will be needed
for a 3 metre wide pond that is 8 metres long?
Show how you worked this out.

C2 (a) Describe how the number of slabs needed goes up as the size
of the pond goes up.

(b) Explain why the number of slabs goes up in this way.

▽■● **C3** How many slabs are needed for a 3 metre wide pond
that measures 20 metres in length?
Show how you worked out your answer.

▽□● **C4** Which of these gives how many slabs are needed for
a 3 metre wide rectangular pond that is x metres long?

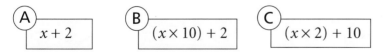

Ⓐ $x + 2$ Ⓑ $(x \times 10) + 2$ Ⓒ $(x \times 2) + 10$

▽□● **C5** Investigate different sets of rectangular ponds.
Explain any patterns you notice.

D Earrings

Chris is designing earrings with red and yellow beads.

How many different
three-bead earrings
can he make?

D1 How many different two-bead earrings can he make?

D2 Copy and complete the table.

Number of beads	1	2	3
Number of different earrings			

D3 (a) How many different four-bead earrings do you think can be made?

(b) Show how you found your answer.

(c) Check it by finding the different earrings.

D4 How many different five-bead earrings do you think can be made?

▽□● **D5** (a) Describe how the number of different earrings goes up.

(b) Try to explain why the numbers go up like this.

E Staircases   ▽■●

In this activity you can climb one step at a time or
two steps at a time.

This staircase has 4 steps.
The diagram below shows one way to climb it.

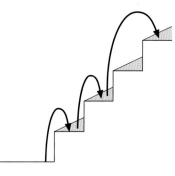

E1 Find all the ways of climbing this staircase.
How many different ways are there?

E2 Find all the different ways of climbing a staircase with

(a) 5 steps   (b) 3 steps

E3 Copy and complete this table.

Number of steps	1	2	3	4	5
Number of different ways					

E4 (a) How many different ways do you think there are
to climb a staircase with 6 steps?

(b) Show how you found your answer.

(c) Check it by finding all the different ways of climbing 6 steps.

E5 Describe how the number of different ways to climb
the staircases goes up.

▽□● E6 Try to explain why the numbers go up in this way.

What progress have you made?

Statement

▼■● I can find, use and explain patterns.

Evidence

Carol is planning a display of yellow and red rose bushes. Some designs for her display are shown below.

1 How many yellow rose bushes are needed for

(a) 2 red rose bushes

(b) 4 red rose bushes

2 Draw Carol's design for 3 red rose bushes.

3 Copy and complete this table for Carol's designs.

Number of red bushes	1	2	3	4	5
Number of yellow bushes					

4 (a) How many yellow bushes will be needed for 8 red bushes?

(b) Show how you worked this out.

5 (a) How does the number of yellow bushes go up as the number of red bushes goes up?

(b) Explain why the number of yellow bushes goes up in this way.

▽■● 6 (a) How many yellow bushes will be needed for 100 red bushes?

(b) Show how you worked this out.

▽□● 7 (a) How many **red** bushes will be needed for 50 **yellow** bushes?

(b) Show how you worked this out.

 # Angle

This work will help you

◆ understand right angles, acute, obtuse and reflex angles

◆ measure angles

◆ calculate angles

A Making angles ▼■●

Practical work is described in the teacher's guide.

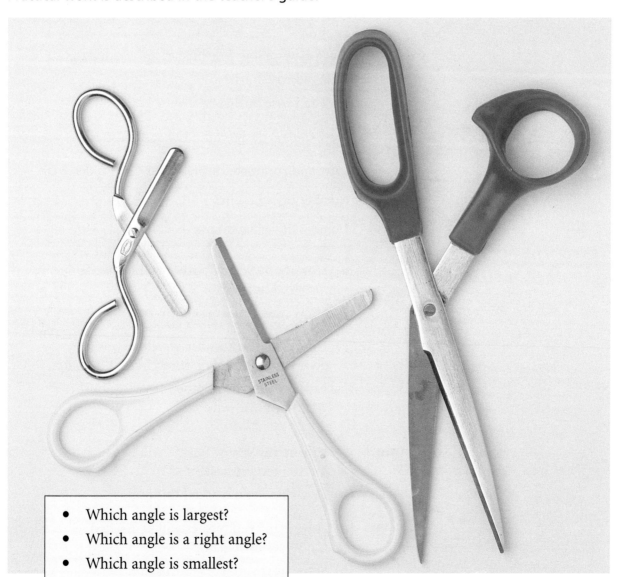

- Which angle is largest?
- Which angle is a right angle?
- Which angle is smallest?

B Comparing angles

You need tracing paper.

B1 Trace angle *X*.
Use your tracing to find which of the other angles are bigger
than *X* and which are smaller.

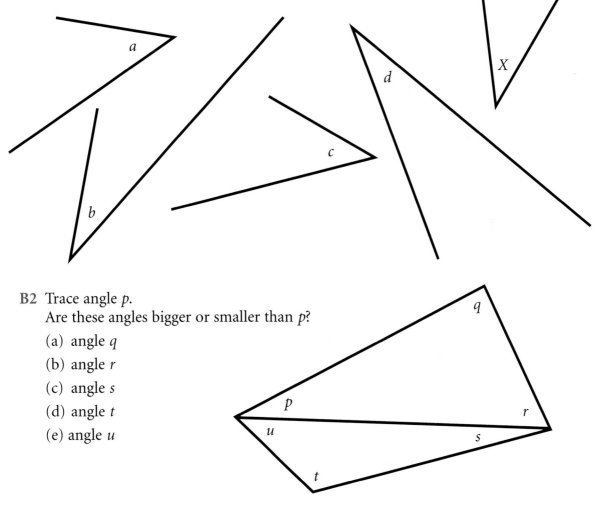

B2 Trace angle *p*.
Are these angles bigger or smaller than *p*?

(a) angle *q*

(b) angle *r*

(c) angle *s*

(d) angle *t*

(e) angle *u*

B3 Put these angles in order of size, smallest first.
Use tracings if you need to, but try to do without.

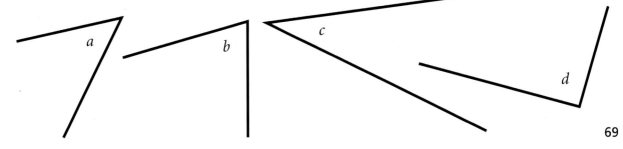

C Right angles, acute, obtuse and reflex angles

An **angle** is made when a line turns from one position to another.

As the line turns, so the angle gets bigger … and bigger … and bigger …

… until the line has made a **full turn**.

full turn

Each of these angles is a **half turn**.

half turn

half turn

Each of these is a **quarter turn**.

quarter turn

quarter turn

quarter turn

quarter turn

A quarter turn is also called a **right angle**.

A right angle

The symbol for a right angle is a little square.

Angles that are smaller than a right angle are called **acute** angles.

Acute angles

Angles that are bigger than a right angle (but less than two right angles) are called **obtuse** angles.

Obtuse angles

Angles that are bigger than two right angles are called **reflex** angles.

Reflex angles

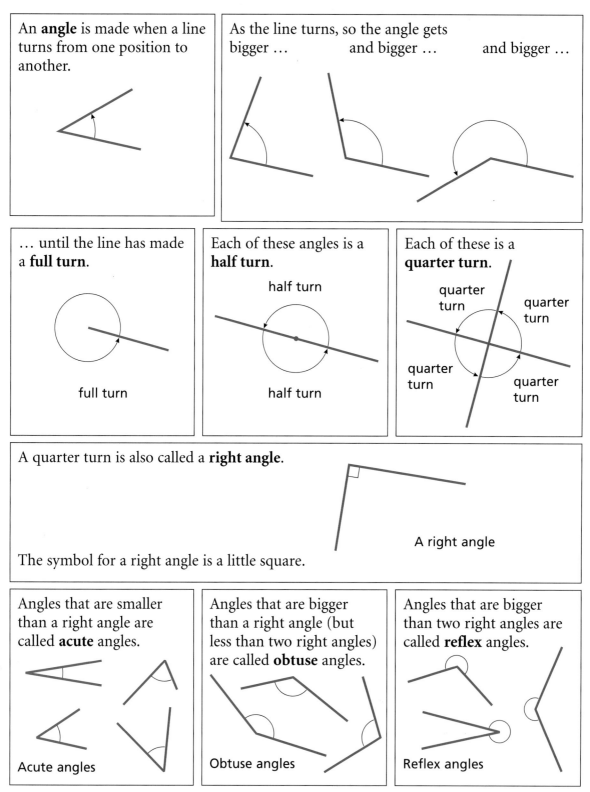

70

C1 Which of the angles *a*, *b*, *c*, *d*, *e*, *f* are right angles? You can use the corner of a piece of paper to check.

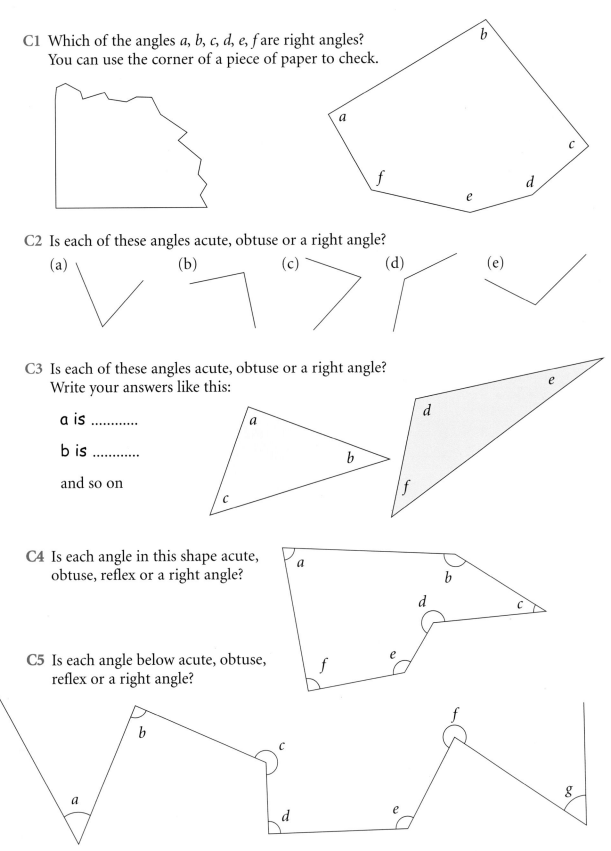

C2 Is each of these angles acute, obtuse or a right angle?

(a)　　　　(b)　　　　(c)　　　　(d)　　　　(e)

C3 Is each of these angles acute, obtuse or a right angle? Write your answers like this:

a is ....

b is ....

and so on

C4 Is each angle in this shape acute, obtuse, reflex or a right angle?

C5 Is each angle below acute, obtuse, reflex or a right angle?

71

D Measuring angles

▼■●

Angles are measured in **degrees**.
There are 360 degrees (**360°**) in a full turn.

How to use an angle measurer

Set the red pointer at 0.
Put the centre hole over the point of the angle.

Put the pointer along one arm of the angle.
Then move it round to the other arm.

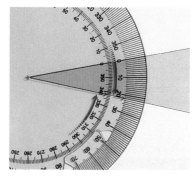

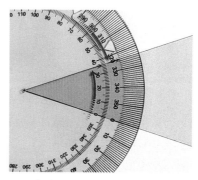

Read the outside scale when the
pointer goes clockwise.

Read the inside scale when the
pointer goes anti-clockwise.

D1 You need sheet 75, 76 or 77.

D2 Without measuring, say if there are any angles here
which look equal to each other.

Then check by measuring.

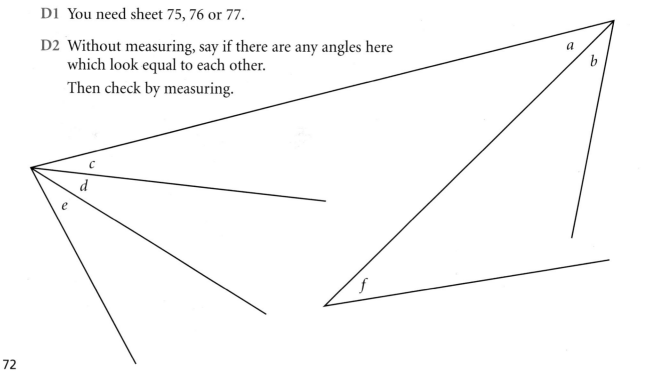

D3 (a) Measure the three angles of this triangle.

(b) Add the three angles together.

(c) Draw a triangle of your own and do the same.
Do you get the same total?

x

y

a

z

D4 (a) Measure the four angles of this shape.

b

(b) Add the four angles together.

(c) Draw a four-sided shape of your own and
do the same. Do you get the same total?

d

c

Tilting bus

This bus is being tested to make sure
it does not tip over easily.

What angle does the pointer on the
front of the bus show?

What angle does the pointer on the
side of the tilting platform show?

Why do you think they are different?

E Drawing angles

▽■●

Using an angle measurer to draw an angle of 130°

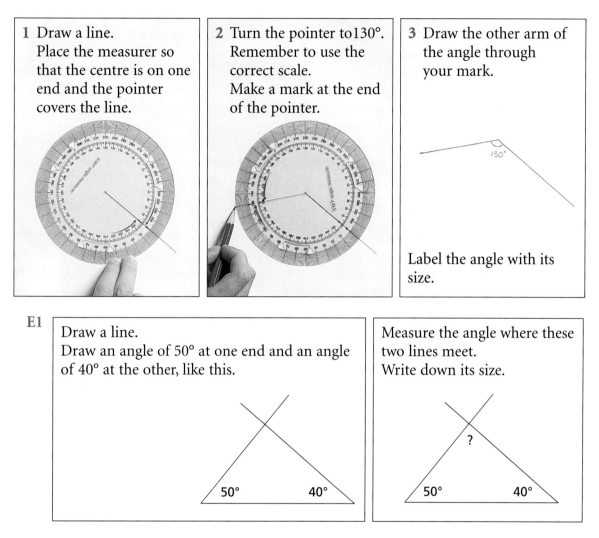

1 Draw a line.
Place the measurer so that the centre is on one end and the pointer covers the line.

2 Turn the pointer to130°.
Remember to use the correct scale.
Make a mark at the end of the pointer.

3 Draw the other arm of the angle through your mark.

Label the angle with its size.

E1

Draw a line.
Draw an angle of 50° at one end and an angle of 40° at the other, like this.

50°   40°

Measure the angle where these two lines meet.
Write down its size.

?

50°   40°

E2 Repeat E1 but with angles of 70° and 60°.

E3 Repeat E1 but with angles of 20° and 120°.

E4 Draw a four-sided shape with three of its angles 40°, 110° and 130°.

(a) Measure the fourth angle of the shape.

(b) Add all four angles together.

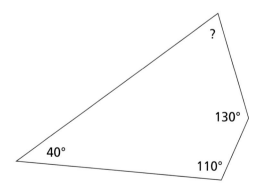

?

40°

130°

110°

F Angles round a point

▽■●

F1 This clock has only an hour hand.
It moves from 1 o'clock to 2 o'clock.
How many degrees does it turn through?

F2 Work out (don't measure!) how many degrees
the hand turns through between

(a) 2 o'clock and 4 o'clock

(b) 8 o'clock and 11 o'clock

(c) 3 o'clock and 8 o'clock

F3 The hand turns like this between 10 o'clock in the
morning and 7 o'clock in the evening.
How many degrees does it turn through?

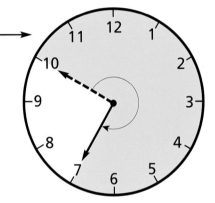

F4 Work out how many degrees the hand turns through
between

(a) 8 a.m. (morning) and 1 p.m. (afternoon)

(b) 8 a.m. and 3 p.m.   (c) 6 a.m. and 3 p.m.

(d) 10 a.m. and 4 p.m.   (e) 7 a.m. and 7 p.m.

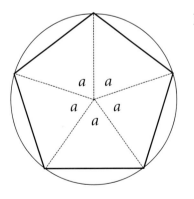

F5 The shape inside the circle is called a **regular pentagon**.
The five angles marked a at the centre of the circle are all
equal.

(a) What do the five angles marked a add up to?

(b) What is the size of each angle marked a?

(c) Draw a circle with compasses.
Draw the five equal angles at the centre of your circle.
Join up the five points on the circle to make your
regular pentagon.

(d) If you have done this accurately, the five sides of your
pentagon should be the same length. Check this.

F6 Choose a regular polygon from this list and draw it inside a circle.

Regular octagon (8 sides)   Regular nonagon (9 sides)

Regular decagon (10 sides)   Regular dodecagon (12 sides)

G Calculating angles

▽■●

Angles round a point

Angles round a point make up a full turn.
So they must add up to **360°**.

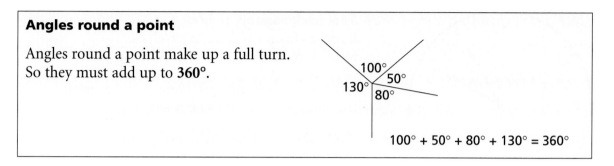

$100° + 50° + 80° + 130° = 360°$

G1 Calculate the angles marked with letters.

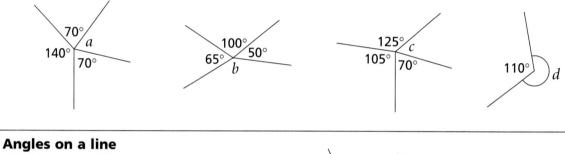

Angles on a line

Angles on a line make a half turn.
So they must add up to **180°**.

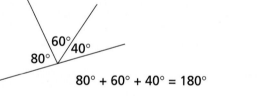

$80° + 60° + 40° = 180°$

G2 Calculate the angles marked with letters.

G3 Calculate the angles marked with letters.

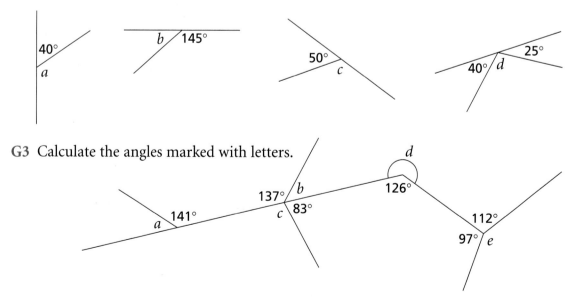

Vertically opposite angles

When a line rotates about a point on it, it makes two pairs of equal angles.

The equal angles in each pair are called **vertically opposite** angles.

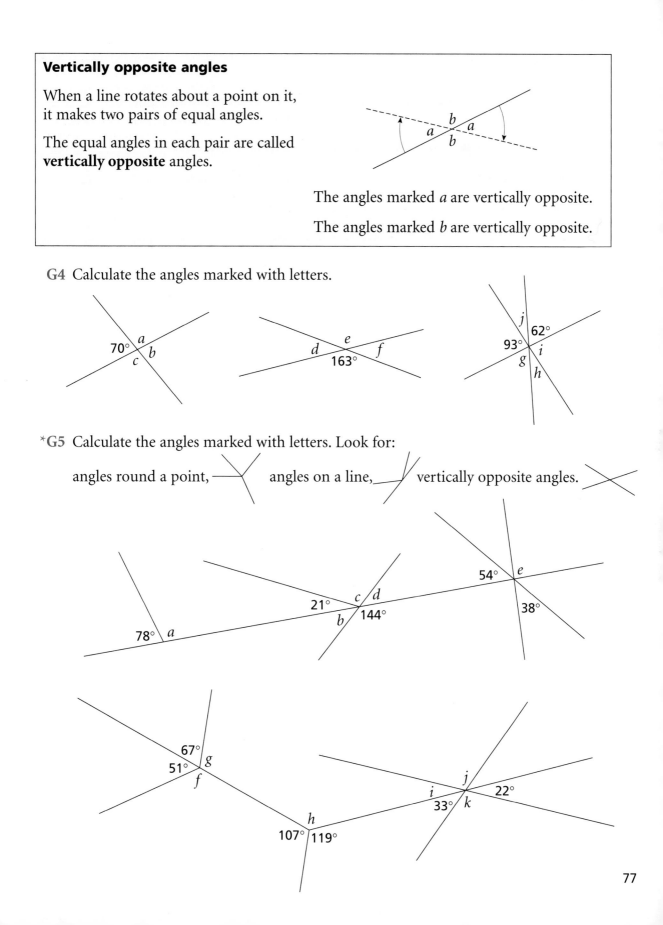

The angles marked *a* are vertically opposite.

The angles marked *b* are vertically opposite.

G4 Calculate the angles marked with letters.

*G5 Calculate the angles marked with letters. Look for:

angles round a point, angles on a line, vertically opposite angles.

77

Imagine that you are walking along in a straight line.	If you turn 20° to your right (or clockwise), your path goes on like this.

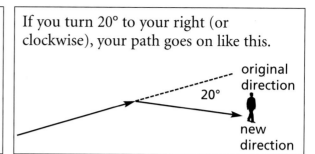

You need sheet 78.

On sheet 78 is a map, with roads, barns and open country.
1 cm stands for 1 km.

Pieces of equipment are hidden in several places.
Follow the instructions below to find them.
When you have found one of them, record its position using coordinates.

Spy camera	**X-ray binoculars**
Start at Pitston Crossroads (4, 2). Walk northwards for 6 km. Turn 50° to your right. Walk for 9 km. The camera is in the nearest barn.	Start at Rowan Crossroads (19, 2). Walk northwards for 5 km. Turn 75° to your left. Walk for 6 km. The binoculars are in the nearest barn.

Coding kit	**Radio**
Start at the south end of the lake. Walk westwards for 3 km. Turn 45° to your right. Walk for 6 km. Turn 80° to your right. Walk for 4 km. The coding kit is in the nearest barn.	Start at Pitston Crossroads facing north. Turn 62° to the right and walk. Meanwhile another person starts at Rowan Crossroads facing north. She turns 25° to the right and walks. The radio is in the barn nearest to where your two paths cross.

Now 'hide' something yourself on the map.
Write instructions to find it.
Give them to a partner and see if they get to the right place.

What progress have you made?

Statement

Evidence

▼□○ I know what right angles, acute
 ↓   angles and obtuse angles are.

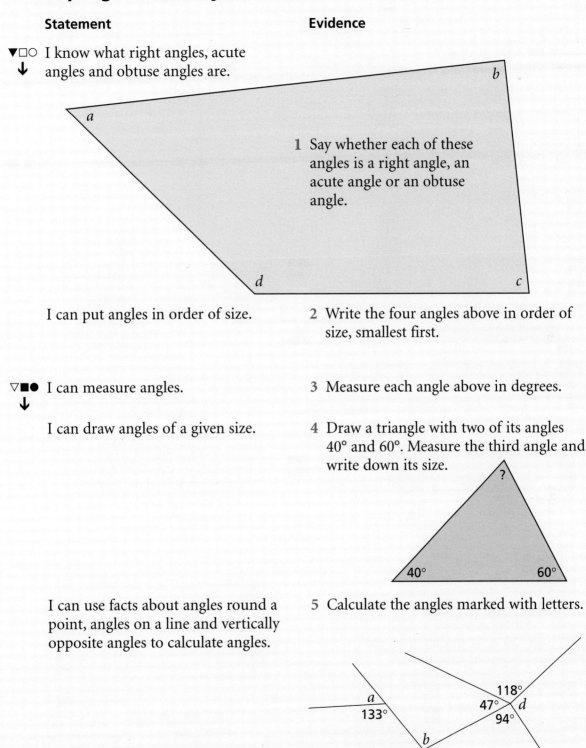

1 Say whether each of these
angles is a right angle, an
acute angle or an obtuse
angle.

I can put angles in order of size.

2 Write the four angles above in order of
size, smallest first.

▽■● I can measure angles.
 ↓

3 Measure each angle above in degrees.

I can draw angles of a given size.

4 Draw a triangle with two of its angles
40° and 60°. Measure the third angle and
write down its size.

I can use facts about angles round a
point, angles on a line and vertically
opposite angles to calculate angles.

5 Calculate the angles marked with letters.

79

Balancing

This work will help you

- ◆ solve simple balance puzzles
- ◆ form equations from balance puzzles
- ◆ solve simple equations with the unknown on both sides

A Scales

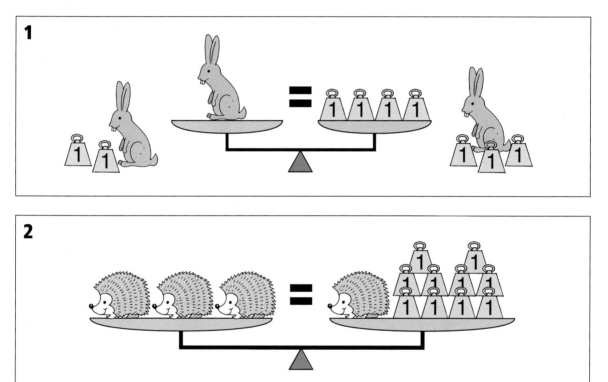

B Balance pictures ▼□○

The scales balance in these pictures.
Find the weight of each animal.

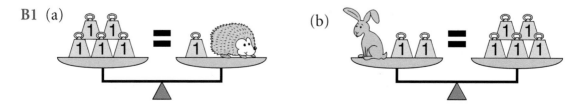

B1 (a)   (b)

B2 These scales balance.
Find the weight of each animal.

(a)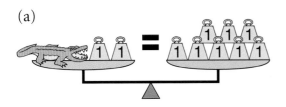

(b)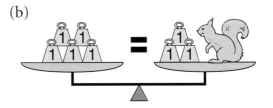

(c)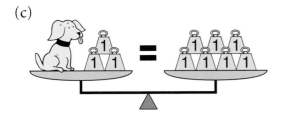

(d)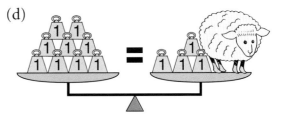

(e)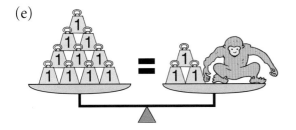

(f)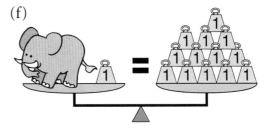

(g)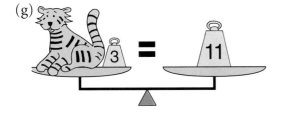

(h)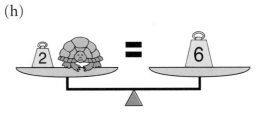

(i)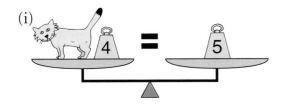

(j)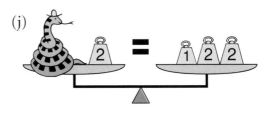

81

B3 Each sack on this balance weighs the same. How many kilograms does each sack weigh?

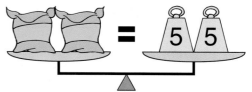

B4 Work out the weight of each of these objects.

(a)

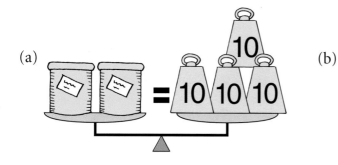

(b)

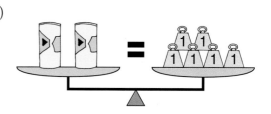

(c)

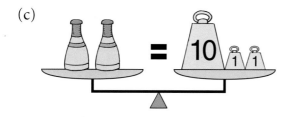

(d)

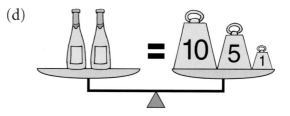

(e)

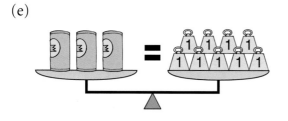

(f)

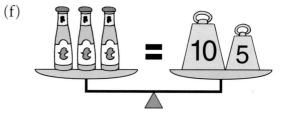

B5 Find the weight of one of these sacks.
(Hint: try taking a sack off each side.)

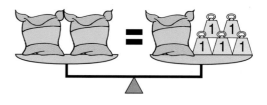

B6 Find the weight of a tin in each of these pictures.

(a)

(b)

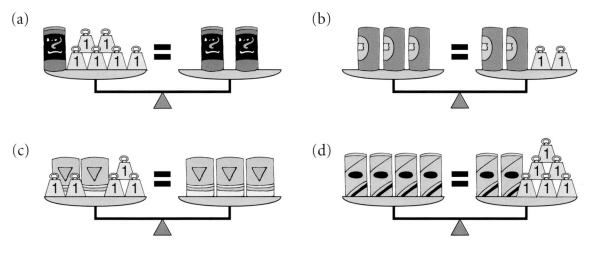

(c)

(d)

B7 Find the weight of one of these tins.
(Hint: first you need to take some
weights off each side.)

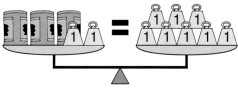

B8 Find the weight of a tin in each of these pictures.

(a)

(b)

(c)

(d)

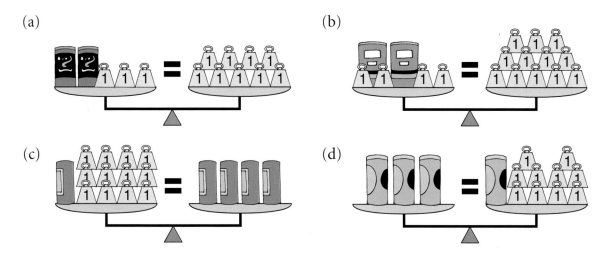

B9 Make up a balance puzzle picture and give it
to someone else to solve.

B10 Draw a balance puzzle picture, and write out an explanation
of how you solve it.

You may want to make a poster of your explanation.

C Writing

To show other people what you are doing when you solve a
balance puzzle, you need a way of writing down your working.

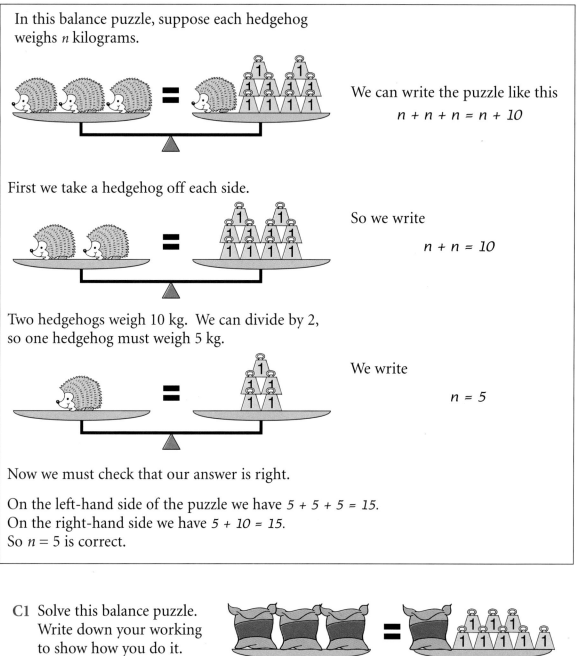

In this balance puzzle, suppose each hedgehog
weighs n kilograms.

We can write the puzzle like this
$$n + n + n = n + 10$$

First we take a hedgehog off each side.

So we write
$$n + n = 10$$

Two hedgehogs weigh 10 kg. We can divide by 2,
so one hedgehog must weigh 5 kg.

We write
$$n = 5$$

Now we must check that our answer is right.

On the left-hand side of the puzzle we have $5 + 5 + 5 = 15$.
On the right-hand side we have $5 + 10 = 15$.
So $n = 5$ is correct.

C1 Solve this balance puzzle.
Write down your working
to show how you do it.

Start by writing $n + n + n = n + 8$

Check your answer.

C2 The tins on this balance all weigh the same.
Find out the weight of a tin.

Write down your working.
Use x to stand for the weight of one tin.

Check your answer.

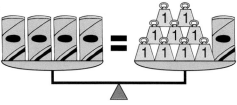

C3 Find out the weight of each animal in these puzzles.
Show your working.
You can choose any letter you like to stand for the
weight of one animal.

Make sure you check each of your answers.

(a)

(b)

(c)

(d)

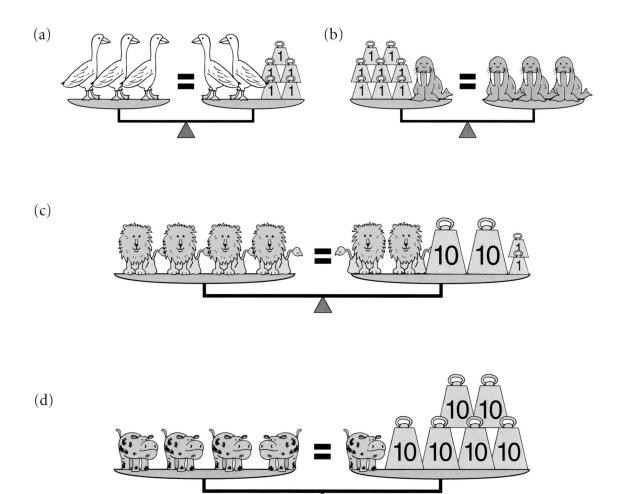

D Weights and objects on both sides

Here we have weights and objects on both sides.

Suppose each ostrich weighs n kg.

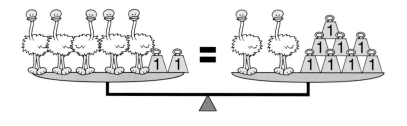

We can write the puzzle as

$$n + n + n + n + n + 2 = n + n + 8$$

We can take ns or numbers off each side.

First we'll take two ns off. So we get

$$n + n + n + 2 = 8$$

Now we have a puzzle like the ones we solved before.

D1 Solve the ostrich balance puzzle to find n. Check your answer works.

D2 Solve each of the balance puzzles below. Write down your working for each one.

Check your answer works for each puzzle.

(a)

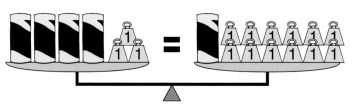

(b)

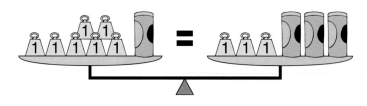

(c)

D3 Solve each of these puzzles, showing your working.
Check your answers work.

(a)

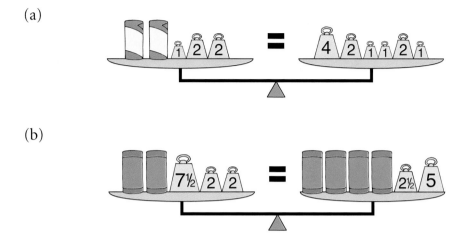

(b)

D4 Here is a balance puzzle. $s + s + s + 6 = s + 12$
Draw a picture for the puzzle.

Then solve the puzzle and check
your answer works.

D5 Solve these balance puzzles.
Show all your working and check that each answer works.
You do not need to draw pictures.

(a) $y + y + y + y = y + y + 24$

(b) $p + p + p + 5 = p + p + 8$

(c) $z + 10 + z = z + 12$

(d) $g + g + 5 = g + g + g + g$

(e) $n + n + n + n + 15 = n + 33$

(f) $t + t + t + t + t + 12 = t + 18 + t + t$

(g) $22 + w + w = 18 + w + w + w + w$

(h) $15 + d = 10 + d + d + d$

(i) $b + b + b + 100 = b + b + 120$

(j) $k + 17 + k + 10 + k = k + 32 + k$

D6 Make up a balance puzzle and give it to a friend to solve.
(Make sure you can solve it yourself first!)

E Using shorthand

Here we have weights and objects on both sides.

Suppose each ostrich weighs n kg.

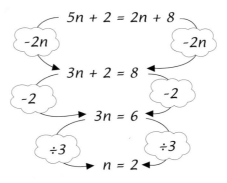

We can write the puzzle as

$$n + n + n + n + n + 2 = n + n + 8$$

A shorter way to write the puzzle is

We can take ns or numbers off each side. First we'll take $2n$ off. So we get

Now we can take 2 off each side.

$$5n + 2 = 2n + 8$$

$-2n$ $-2n$

$$3n + 2 = 8$$

-2 -2

$$3n = 6$$

Lastly we can divide both sides by 3.

$÷3$ $÷3$

$$n = 2$$

E1 Check that $n = 2$ fits the ostrich puzzle.

E2 Solve each of the balance puzzles below.
Write down your working for each one.
Write it in shorthand, like in the example above.

Check your answer works for each puzzle.

(a)

(b)

(c)

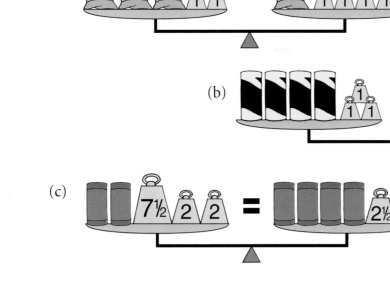

88

E3 Solve these puzzles.
Show your working and check your answers.

(a)

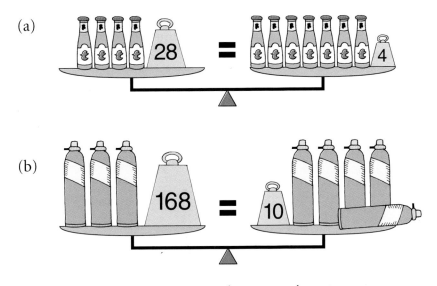

(b)

E4 Here is a balance puzzle.   *3h + 15 = h + 37*
Draw a picture for the puzzle.

Then solve the puzzle and check
your answer works.

E5 Solve these balance puzzles.
Show all your working and check that each answer works.
You do not have to draw pictures.

(a) *4p + 20 = p + 41*   (b) *6d = 2d + 24*

(c) *3s + 70 = 10s + 14*   (d) *2q + 20 = 4q*

(e) *3n + 21 = 8n + 1*   (f) *5u + 12 = u + 118 + 2u*

(g) *23 + 4k = 8k + 13*   (h) *7y + 11 = 10 + 10y*

(i) *20a + 35 = 100 + 7a*   (j) *3w + 7 = 6 + 5w*

(k) *220 + 2b = 180 + 4b*   (l) *100f + 10 = 75f + 90*

(m) *5j + 9 = 60 + 2j*   (n) *8 + 10s = 10 + 9s*

*E6 See if you can solve these balance puzzles.

(a) *10 + d = 15 + ½d*   (b) *2½e + 10 = 4e + 1*

(c) *0.1 k + 1 = 1.1 k + 0.1*   (d) *6y + ⁻2 = 4y + 5*

E7 Make up a balance puzzle and give it to a friend to solve.
(Make sure you can solve it yourself first!)

What progress have you made?

Statement

▼□○ I can solve a picture balance puzzle.

▽■○ I can solve balance puzzles using letters.

▽□● I can solve balance puzzles using shorthand.

Evidence

1 Find the weight of a goose in this picture.

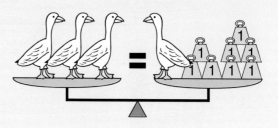

2 Draw a balance puzzle of your own and then solve it.

3 Solve these balance puzzles.
  (a) $w + w + w + 10 = w + w + 21$
  (b) $d + d + d + d + 12 = d + d + 30$
  (c) $k + 20 = 10 + k + k + k$

4 Draw a picture for this balance puzzle.
  $10 + t = t + t + t + 2$
  Solve the puzzle.

5 Solve these balance puzzles.
  (a) $3y + 12 = y + 20$
  (b) $40 + 2h = 5h + 1$
  (c) $20 + 2f = 5 + 5f$
  (d) $8w + 40 = 100 + 3w$

6 Draw a picture for this balance puzzle. Then solve the puzzle.
  $12 + 2q = q + 21$

Review 2

▼■●
↓

1 Zoe is making displays of purple and yellow tulips.
   Here are some of her displays.

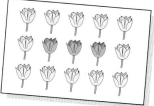

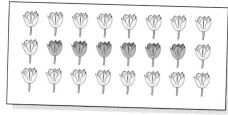

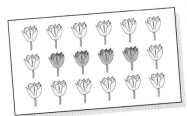

How many yellow tulips are needed for

(a) 5 purple tulips   (b) 1 purple tulip

2 Draw Zoe's display for 2 purple tulips.

3 Copy and complete this table for Zoe's displays.

Number of purple tulips	1	2	3	4	5	6
Number of yellow tulips						

4 (a) Without drawing, how many yellow tulips
       would be needed for a display with 10 purples?

  (b) One display needs 30 **yellow** tulips.
       How many purple tulips are there?

5 (a) How does the number of yellow tulips go up
       as the number of purples goes up?

  (b) Explain why the number of yellow tulips goes up in this way.

▽■● 6 (a) How many yellow tulips would be needed for 20 purples?

  (b) Show how you worked this out.

▽□● 7 Suppose the number of purple tulips in one display is n.
   Which of these tells you the number of yellow tulips?

$n + 6$

$(n \times 2) + 6$

$n \times 8$

$n \times 2$

$(n \times 6) + 2$

$(n \times 2) + 4$

8

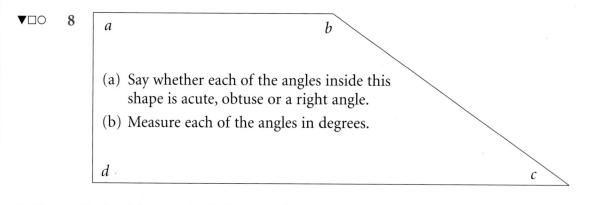

   (a) Say whether each of the angles inside this shape is acute, obtuse or a right angle.

   (b) Measure each of the angles in degrees.

▼■○   **9** Each of these scales balances. The weights are in kilograms. Find the weight of a tin in each picture.

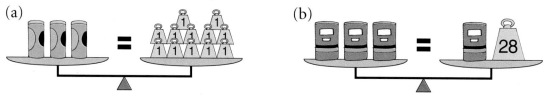

(a)   (b)

▽■●   **10** (a) Look at question 9(a).

            Suppose that *n* stands for the weight of a tin in kilograms.

            Write down the balance puzzle using *n*.
            Solve the puzzle. Show your working and check your answer.

    (b) Choose your own letter for the weight of a tin in question 9(b). Solve the puzzle and show your working.

  11 (a) Draw a five-sided shape with four of its angles 80°, 165°, 90° and 120°.

    (b) Measure the fifth angle.

    (c) Add all five angles together.

  12 Calculate each angle marked with a letter.

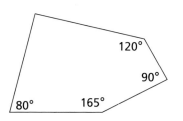

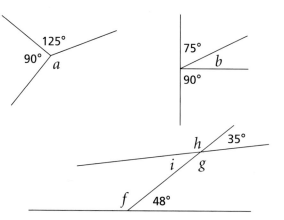

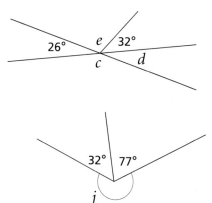

Health club

This is about looking at data.
The work will help you

◆ find medians and compare sets of data

◆ draw and interpret dot plots and bar charts

A On record   ▼■●

The introduction is described in the teacher's guide.

04 ARCHES Health Club

K Berris   M Ⓕ

Age group	Height
11–20	146 cm
Weight	**Rest pulse**
39 kg	52 bpm

01 ARCHES Health Club

J Abram   Ⓜ F

Age group	Height
31–40	183 cm
Weight	**Rest pulse**
88 kg	82 bpm

Health Club
                                 M Ⓕ

Height
180 cm
Rest pulse
78 bpm

Weight
70 kg

A1 How heavy is S Anderson?

A2 What is F Trudeau's rest pulse?

A3 How tall is L Unwin?

A4 Name two people who are over 170 cm tall.

A5 Who has the lowest weight?
What is their weight?

A6 How many people are in the 21–30 age group?

A7 Who is the tallest person?

A8 Two people have a rest pulse of 60 bpm.
Who are they?

A9 List the names of all the people whose heights are under 160 cm.

A10 How many people are over 30 years of age?

A11 Find the female with the highest resting pulse rate.

A12 How many males are heavier than 70 kg?

A13 How many people in the 31–40 age group have
a pulse rate less than 70 bpm?

A14 List the names of the men who are
lighter than 75 kg and also taller than 170 cm.

B On display ▼■●

The introductory activity is described in the teacher's guide.

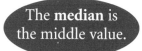

The **median** is
the middle value.

B1 Arrange the set of cards in order of weight.
Find the median weight.

B2 Draw a dot plot for the weights on sheet 83.

B3 Draw a grouped bar chart for the weights on sheet 83.

B4 What do the dot plot and bar chart show about the
weights of people at the club?

B5 (a) Find the median rest pulse rate.

(b) Draw a dot plot for the rest pulse rates on sheet 83.

(c) Draw a grouped bar chart for the rest pulse rates on sheet 83.

(d) What do the dot plot and bar chart show about the rest pulse rates
of people at the club?

▽□● **B6** (a) Explain why you cannot find the median age of people at the
Arches health club if you only have the information on the cards.

(b) Which of these could be the median age of the people at the club?

12 years   18 years   23 years   30 years   32 years   39 years   45 years

Explain how you decided.

▽□● **B7** This bar chart gives information about the ages of the people at the Fit for Life club.

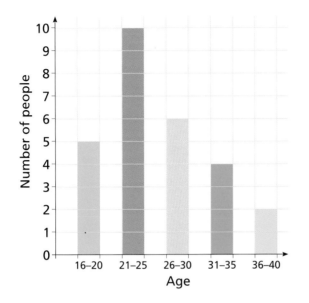

Which of these could be the median age of the people at the club?

20 years   22 years   25 years   30 years   31 years

Explain how you decided.

▽□● **B8** These cards are for eight women at the Fit for Life club.

Fit for Life Club	
K Smith	M Ⓕ
Age group	16–20
Height	166 cm
Weight	54 kg
Rest pulse	60 bpm

Fit for Life Club	
T Cheung	M Ⓕ
Age group	21–25
Height	158 cm
Weight	61 kg
Rest pulse	63 bpm

Fit for Life Club	
Y Waters	M Ⓕ
Age group	26–30
Height	168 cm
Weight	64 kg
Rest pulse	65 bpm

Fit for Life Club	
P Short	M Ⓕ
Age group	16–20
Height	163 cm
Weight	56 kg
Rest pulse	75 bpm

Fit for Life Club	
J Brown	M Ⓕ
Age group	26–30
Height	171 cm
Weight	71 kg
Rest pulse	83 bpm

Fit for Life Club	
M Willox	M Ⓕ
Age group	31–35
Height	175 cm
Weight	83 kg
Rest pulse	80 bpm

Fit for Life Club	
P Patel	M Ⓕ
Age group	26–30
Height	174 cm
Weight	74 kg
Rest pulse	72 bpm

Fit for Life Club	
L Sayers	M Ⓕ
Age group	21–25
Height	161 cm
Weight	57 kg
Rest pulse	66 bpm

What do you think is (a) the median height (b) the median weight of these women?

C Males and females

The introductory activity is described in the teacher's guide.

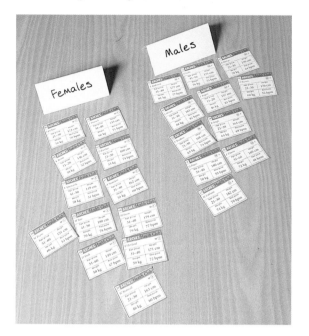

C1 (a) Sort the cards into two sets: males and females.

   (b) Arrange each set in order of weight.

   (c) Find the median weight for the males.

   (d) Find the median weight for females.

   (e) What do the medians suggest about the weights of males and females at the Arches health club?

C2 (a) Draw dot plots for the weights of males and the weights of females on sheet 86.

   (b) Draw grouped bar charts for the weights of males and of females on sheet 86.

   (c) What do the dot plots and grouped bar charts suggest about the weights of males and females at the club?

C3 (a) Find the median rest pulse for the males and the median rest pulse for the females.

   (b) Draw dot plots for the rest pulses of males and females on sheet 87.

   (c) Draw grouped bar charts for the rest pulses of males and females on sheet 87.

   (d) What do the medians, dot plots and grouped bar charts suggest about the rest pulses of males and females at the club?

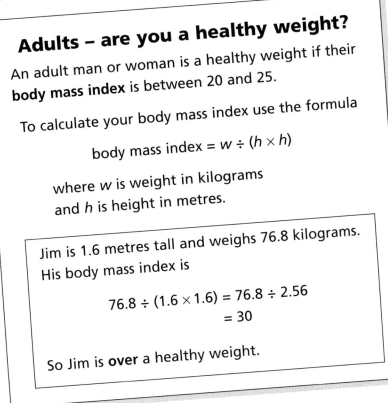

Adults – are you a healthy weight?

An adult man or woman is a healthy weight if their **body mass index** is between 20 and 25.

To calculate your body mass index use the formula

$$\text{body mass index} = w \div (h \times h)$$

where w is weight in kilograms
and h is height in metres.

Jim is 1.6 metres tall and weighs 76.8 kilograms. His body mass index is

$$76.8 \div (1.6 \times 1.6) = 76.8 \div 2.56$$
$$= 30$$

So Jim is **over** a healthy weight.

D1 According to this rule, which of the adult males and females are

(a) over a healthy weight

(b) under a healthy weight

What progress have you made?

Statement	Evidence
▼■● I can interpret data.	Your work in section A is evidence of this.
I can find the median of a set of values.	Your work in sections B and C is evidence of this.
I can draw and interpret dot plots and grouped bar charts.	Your work in sections B and C is evidence of this.
I can use medians, dot plots and grouped bar charts to compare two sets of data.	Your work in section C is evidence of this.

11 Triangles

This work will help you

◆ draw triangles with particular lengths and angles

◆ identify special sorts of triangle and use their properties

◆ calculate with angles of a triangle

A Drawing a triangle accurately ▼■●

This is a rough sketch of the triangle you are going to draw.

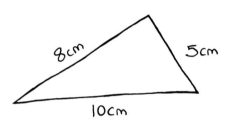

1 Draw the longest side.
Label it with its length.

10 cm

2 Set your compasses so that the sharp point and the pencil point are 8 cm apart.

3 Put the compass point at the end of your line. Draw part of a circle.

10 cm

4 Set your compasses to 5 cm.
Draw part of a circle with its centre at the other end of the line.

10 cm

5 Draw the other two sides of the triangle.

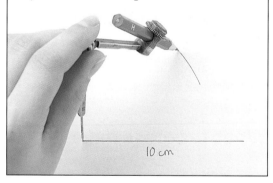

Some new words to use

Part of a circle is called an **arc**.

The distance between the points of a pair of compasses is called the **radius** of the arc or circle you draw.

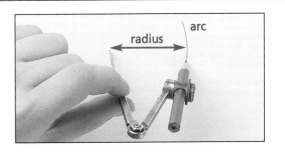

Drawing a shape accurately with a pencil, ruler and compasses is sometimes called **constructing** it. So drawings done this way are called **constructions**.

Another word for the corner of a shape is **vertex**.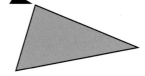

The plural of vertex is **vertices** (pronounced verty-seas).

These are rough sketches of some triangles.
Use the compasses method to construct them on plain paper.
Inside each triangle write its letter. Then cut it out or trace it.

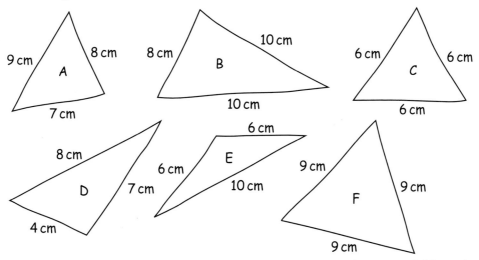

After you have cut or traced your triangles, compare them with your neighbour's.
Does your neighbour's triangle A fit exactly on top of your triangle A?
Try this with all the triangles. (**Then keep them for later.**)

Investigation Try to draw a triangle with sides 10 cm, 4 cm and 5 cm. What happens?
Can you find another three lengths for which the same thing happens?
How can you tell without drawing if three given lengths will make a triangle?

B Equilateral triangles

▼■●

A triangle with three sides the same length is called an **equilateral** triangle.

all sides the
same length

Equilateral triangle

B1 (a) Which of the triangles you drew in section A are equilateral triangles?

(b) Measure their angles. What do you notice?

B2 Does an equilateral triangle have reflection symmetry? Explain how you know.

A design with eight equilateral triangles can be folded up to make a **regular octahedron**.

1 Put an A4 sheet of thin card this way round.
Mark a point A about halfway down and 5 cm in from the left.
Starting from A, draw a line about 20 cm long.

A

2 Set the radius of your compasses to 6 cm.
Starting at point A, mark off three arcs along the line. Label the points B, C, D.

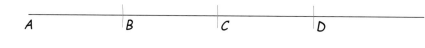

A   B   C   D

3 Put your compass point on points A, B, C and D, and draw arcs above and below the line, like this.

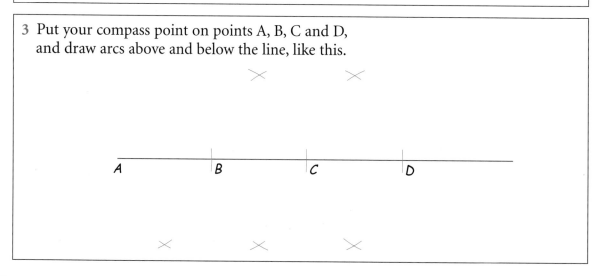

A   B   C   D

4 Draw lines to make
six equilateral triangles.

5 Extend the lines at the top and bottom
of your design and draw arcs for
two more equilateral triangles.

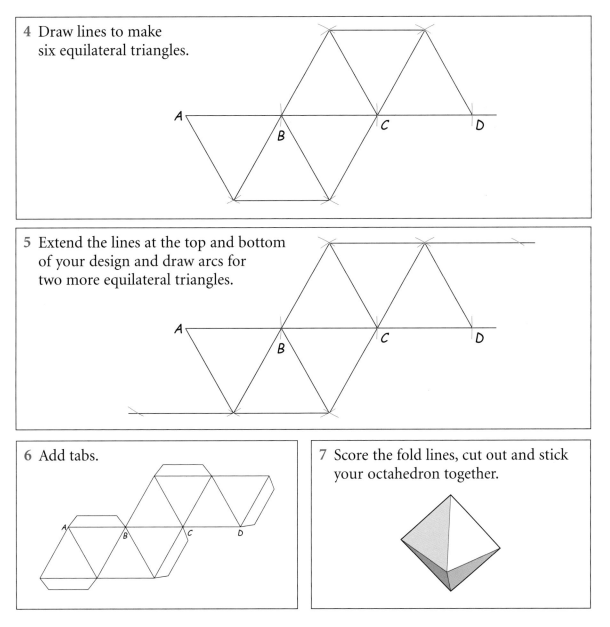

6 Add tabs.

7 Score the fold lines, cut out and stick
your octahedron together.

B3 How many vertices does your octahedron have?

B4 How many edges (folds or joins) does it have?

B5 Why do you think it is called a **regular** octahedron?

Here are some more three-dimensional shapes made from equilateral triangles.
You could work out how to draw and make them.

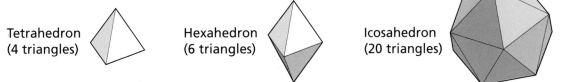

Tetrahedron
(4 triangles)

Hexahedron
(6 triangles)

Icosahedron
(20 triangles)

C Isosceles triangles

▼■●

A triangle with two or more sides the same length
is called an **isosceles** triangle.

two (or more) sides
the same length

Isosceles triangle

C1 Which of the triangles you drew in section A are isosceles?

C2 Fold one of your isosceles triangles so that
two sides the same length come together.
Unfold it.

(a) What can you say about this angle?

(b) What can you say about these angles?

(c) What can you say about the symmetry of an isosceles triangle?

C3 The sides of the pyramids in Egypt
are isosceles triangles.
These are the measurements for
the Great Pyramid at Cheops.

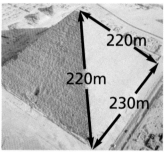

220m

220m

230m

You can make a scale model of it like this.

1 Get sheet 88.
The square on it has sides 9.2 cm long. Set your compasses to 8.8 cm. Use them to draw an isosceles triangle on each side of the square.

2 Add tabs.
Score the folds and cut out the net. Fold it up and stick your pyramid together.

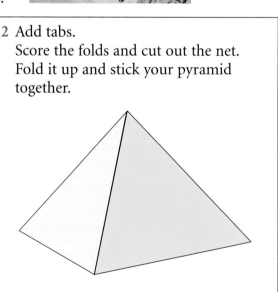

▽■● **C4** How high is your model pyramid?
How did you decide?

▽■● C5 Find all the isosceles triangles in this pattern.
Write them using the letters of their vertices.
For example, triangle NLO is isosceles.

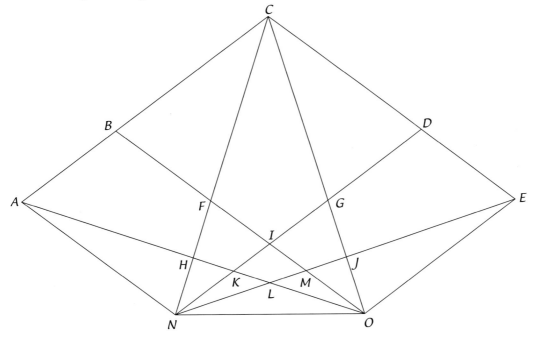

Diagonal cut puzzle

Draw a rectangle.
Draw both diagonals and cut along them.

You now have two pairs of congruent triangles.
What kind of triangles are they?

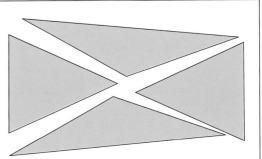

Fit all four pieces together to make one isosceles triangle.

Draw a diagram to show how the pieces fit.

Show how you can fit all four pieces together
to make a different isosceles triangle.

D Scalene triangles

A **scalene** triangle is one that does not have any sides the same length.

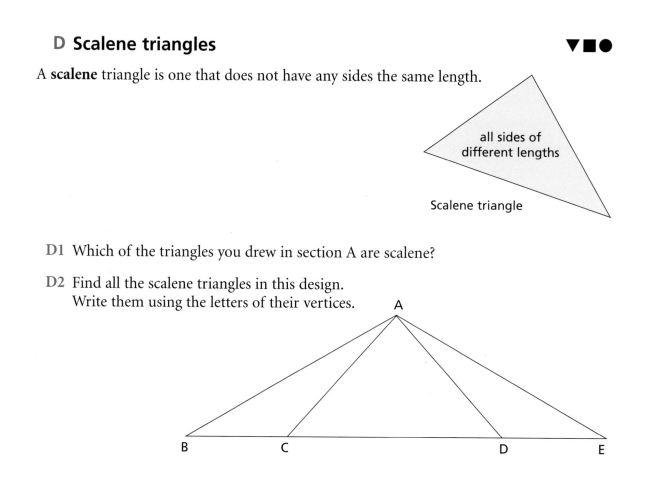

Scalene triangle

D1 Which of the triangles you drew in section A are scalene?

D2 Find all the scalene triangles in this design.
Write them using the letters of their vertices.

D3 For each triangle below, say whether it is equilateral, isosceles or scalene.
(Measure the sides if you need to.)

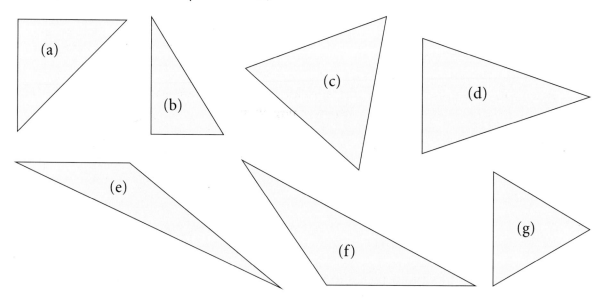

D4 Can a scalene triangle have reflection symmetry? Give a reason.

104

E Using angles

You can draw a triangle if you don't know all three sides.
But you need to know at least one angle.

E1 Follow this method to draw
a triangle with these measurements.

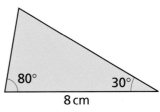

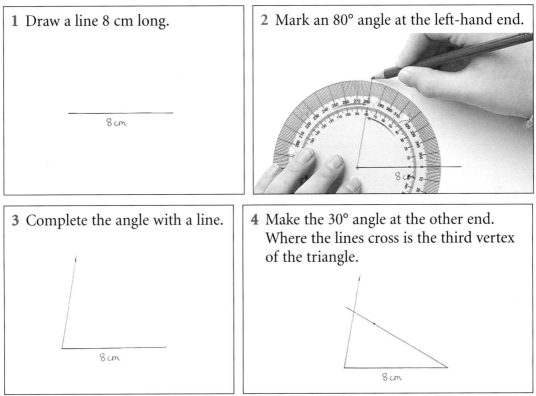

1 Draw a line 8 cm long.	**2** Mark an 80° angle at the left-hand end.
3 Complete the angle with a line.	**4** Make the 30° angle at the other end. Where the lines cross is the third vertex of the triangle.

E2 Use the method to draw these triangles.
After you have done each one, measure **all** the sides and angles.
Compare your measurements with your neighbour's.

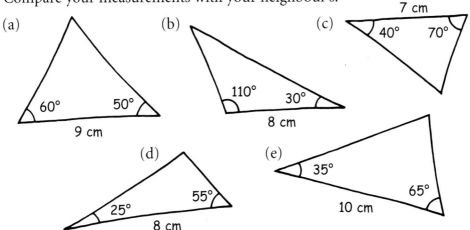

(a)   (b)   (c)

(d)   (e)

105

E3 Try drawing this triangle.

What happens?

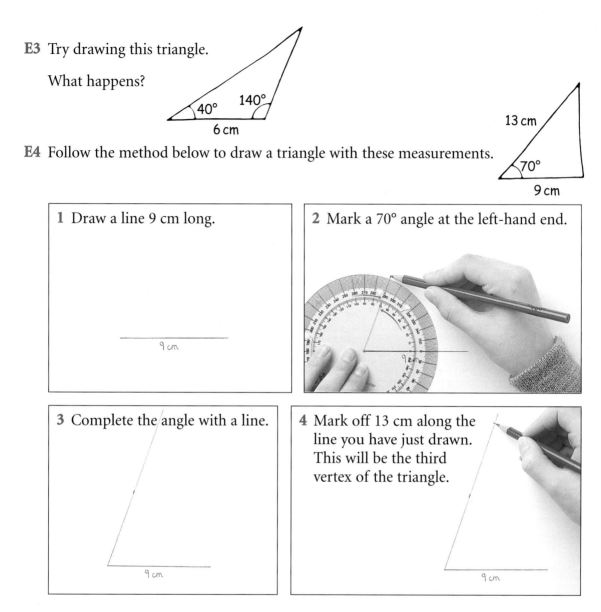

E4 Follow the method below to draw a triangle with these measurements.

1 Draw a line 9 cm long.

9 cm

2 Mark a 70° angle at the left-hand end.

3 Complete the angle with a line.

9 cm

4 Mark off 13 cm along the line you have just drawn. This will be the third vertex of the triangle.

9 cm

E5 Use the method to draw these triangles.
After you have done each one, measure **all** the sides and angles.
Compare your measurements with your neighbour's.

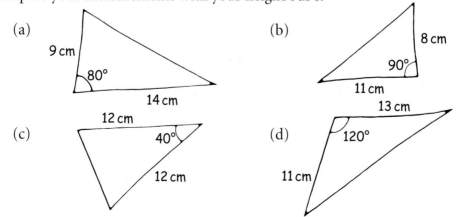

(a) 9 cm 80° 14 cm

(b) 8 cm 90° 11 cm

(c) 12 cm 40° 12 cm

(d) 13 cm 120° 11 cm

E6 (a) Draw this triangle accurately.

(b) Measure the side BC and the angles at B and C.

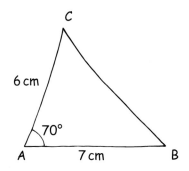

E7 (a) Draw this triangle accurately.

(b) Measure the sides XZ and YZ and the angle at Z.

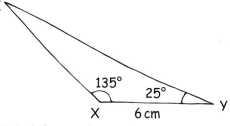

E8 (a) Draw triangle ABC with these measurements. Label the vertices.

     side AB = 7 cm

     side BC = 11 cm

     angle at B = 85°

(b) Measure the side AC and the angles at A and C.

E9 (a) Draw triangle PQR with these measurements. Label the vertices.

     side PR = 8 cm

     side PQ = 6 cm

     angle at P = 125°

(b) Measure the side QR and the angles at Q and R.

▽■● **E10** Try drawing this triangle ABC with a ruler, angle measurer and compasses.

     side AB = 9 cm

     angle at A = 40°

     side BC = 6 cm

What happens?

▽■● **E11** Try drawing this triangle PQR with a ruler, angle measurer and compasses.

     side PQ = 8 cm

     angle at P = 50°

     side QR = 7 cm

What happens?

F Angles of a triangle

1 Draw a triangle.
Measure its angles.

Add them together.

Compare your result with those of others.

2

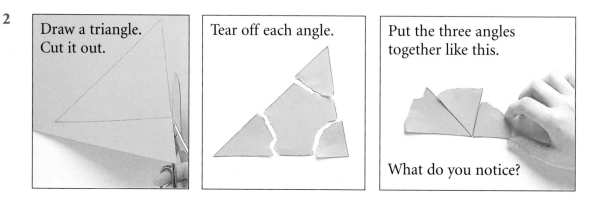

| Draw a triangle. Cut it out. | Tear off each angle. | Put the three angles together like this. What do you notice? |

F1 Work out the angles marked '**?**'.

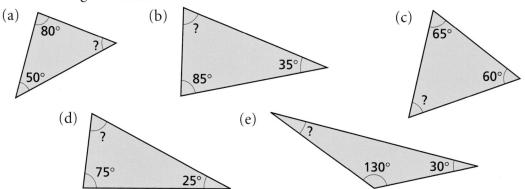

(a) 80°, ?, 50°

(b) ?, 85°, 35°

(c) 65°, 60°, ?

(d) ?, 75°, 25°

(e) ?, 130°, 30°

F2 Work out the angles marked '**?**'.

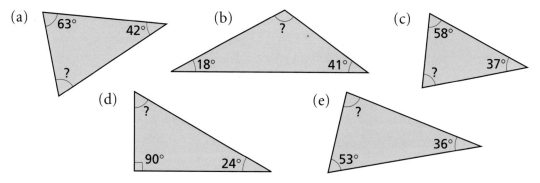

(a) 63°, 42°, ?

(b) ?, 18°, 41°

(c) 58°, ?, 37°

(d) ?, 90°, 24°

(e) ?, 53°, 36°

F3 What are the angles of an equilateral triangle?
Explain how you worked them out.

A triangle with one of its angles 90° is called a **right-angled** triangle.

F4 These are all right-angled triangles.
Work out the angles marked '**?**'.

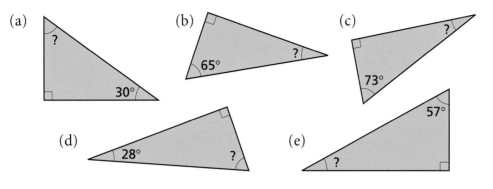

(a)

(b)

(c)

(d)

(e)

F5 Work out the angles marked with letters.

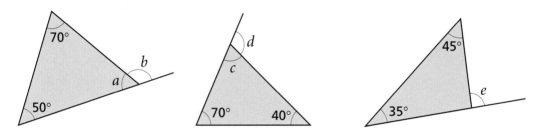

F6 Work out the angles marked with letters.

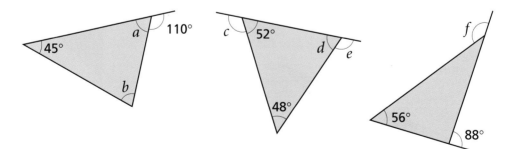

F7 Draw this triangle accurately.

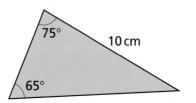

G Using angles in isosceles triangles ▽■●

The equal sides in an isosceles triangle are marked like this.

G1 What can you say about the angles marked *a* and *b* in the triangle above?

G2 Work out the angles marked with letters in these isosceles triangles.

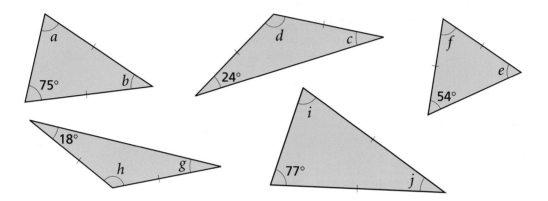

G3 Work out the angles marked with letters in these isosceles triangles.

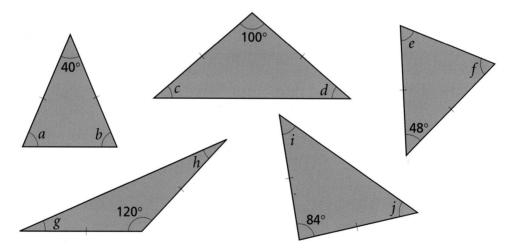

G4 (a) One angle of an isosceles triangle is 40°.
What could the other angles be?

   (b) One angle of an isosceles triangle is 72°.
What could the other angles be?

   (c) One angle of an isosceles triangle is 130°.
What could the other angles be?

G5 Joe has some isosceles triangles all like this.

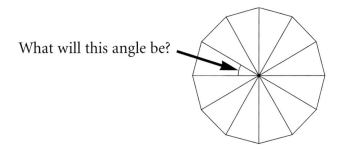

He starts putting them together to try to make a regular polygon.
What will happen?

G6 Carol has some isosceles triangles all like this.
Can she make a regular polygon with them?
Is so, how many sides will the polygon have?

Can you make it?

How can you tell whether you can make a regular polygon if
you know the angles of the isosceles triangle you are using?

How can you work out the number of sides you will get?

G7 Imran wants to make a regular polygon with 12 sides.

What will this angle be?

▽□● **G8** Liz makes this regular polygon with 10 sides.
What will this angle be?

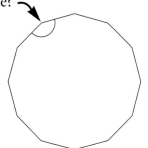

111

What progress have you made?

Statement

▼■●   I can construct a triangle if I know
 ↓   the lengths of its three sides.

I can identify equilateral, isosceles,
scalene and right-angled triangles.

I can draw a triangle accurately
given lengths and angles.

▽■●   I can calculate angles in a triangle.
 ↓

I can calculate with angles in an
isosceles triangle.

Evidence

1 Construct this triangle.

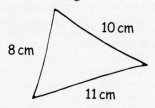

2 Which triangles in this pattern are

   (a) equilateral   (b) isosceles

   (c) scalene   (d) right-angled

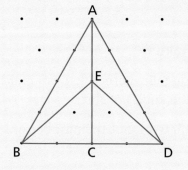

3 Draw these triangles accurately.

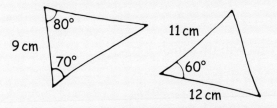

4 Calculate the angles marked with letters.

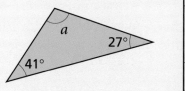

5 Calculate the lettered angles.

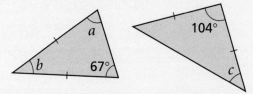

⑫ Work to rule

This is about finding rules for tile designs.
The work will help you find and use rules.

A Mobiles ▼■●

Tom designs mobiles.
He makes the pieces with square glass tiles.

Tom uses a different design for the pieces in this mobile.

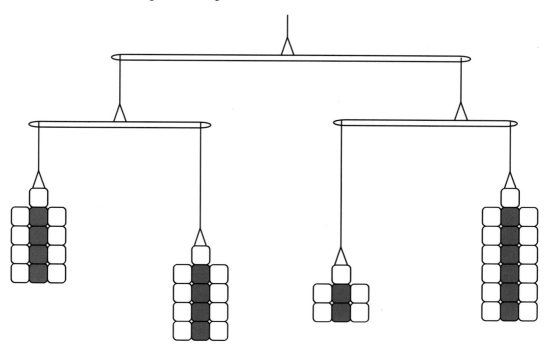

Questions A1 to A14 are all about the mobile above.

A1 Look at the piece that has 2 red tiles.
How many white tiles does it have?

A2 (a) Draw a piece that uses 3 red tiles.

(b) How many white tiles does it have?

A3 (a) Draw a piece that uses 5 red tiles.

(b) How many white tiles does it have?

A4 Copy and complete this table.

Number of red tiles	1	2	3	4	5	6
Number of white tiles				9		

A5 (a) Describe how the number of white tiles goes up
as the number of red tiles goes up.

(b) Explain why the number of white tiles goes up in this way.

114

A6 How many white tiles would you need for a piece with

(a) 8 red tiles   (b) 10 red tiles

A7 How many white tiles would you need for a piece that has 100 red tiles?

A8 Explain how you can find the number of white tiles if you know the number of red tiles.

A9 Work out how many white tiles you would need for a piece with 150 red tiles.

▽■● **A10** Which of these rules describes the link between the number of red tiles and the number of white tiles?

number of white tiles = (number of red tiles × 3) + 1

number of white tiles = number of red tiles + 2

number of white tiles = (number of red tiles × 2) + 2

number of white tiles = (number of red tiles × 2) + 1

number of white tiles = (number of red tiles × 3) + 2

▽■● **A11** Use the rule to work out how many white tiles you would need for

(a) 24 red tiles   (b) 72 red tiles

▽■● **A12** A piece in the mobile has 19 **white** tiles. How many **red** tiles does it have?

▽■● **A13** How many red tiles would you need for a piece that uses 81 white tiles?

▽■● **A14** Explain why it not possible to make a piece that uses 20 white tiles.

115

B Explaining

Here are some pieces from a mobile.

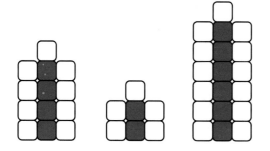

Sushma explained how she found a rule for these pieces, like this.

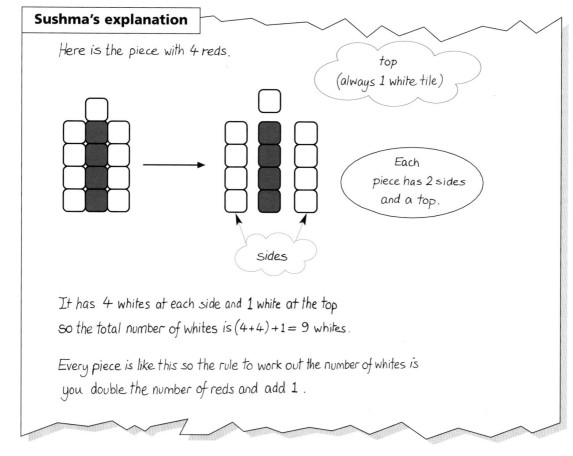

Sushma's explanation

Here is the piece with 4 reds.

top
(always 1 white tile)

Each
piece has 2 sides
and a top.

sides

It has 4 whites at each side and 1 white at the top
so the total number of whites is (4 + 4) + 1 = 9 whites.

Every piece is like this so the rule to work out the number of whites is
you double the number of reds and add 1.

B1 (a) Do you find Sushma's explanation easy to follow?
  (b) Did you find the rule for these pieces in the same way?

Tracy wrote her explanation like this.

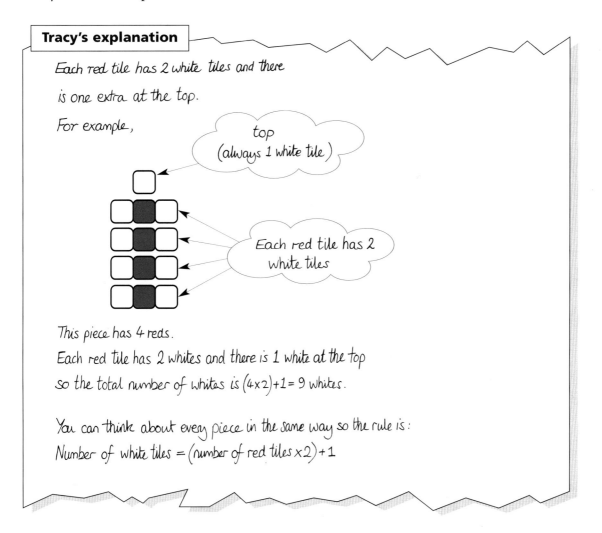

Tracy's explanation

Each red tile has 2 white tiles and there
is one extra at the top.

For example,

top
(always 1 white tile)

Each red tile has 2
white tiles

This piece has 4 reds.
Each red tile has 2 whites and there is 1 white at the top
so the total number of whites is (4×2)+1 = 9 whites.

You can think about every piece in the same way so the rule is:
Number of white tiles = (number of red tiles ×2)+1

B2 Do you find Tracy's explanation easy to follow?

B3 Which explanation did you find easier to follow?
Try to explain why you found it easier to follow.

C Towers and L-shapes

Tom designs pieces for a different mobile.
He calls them 'towers'.

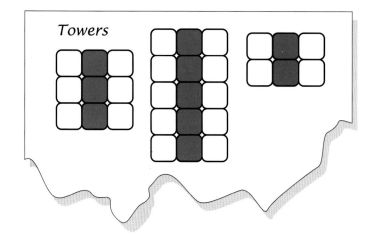

Towers

C1 How many white tiles are used for the piece with 5 red tiles?

C2 (a) Draw a tower that uses 6 red tiles.

(b) How many white tiles does it have?

C3 Copy and complete this table.

Towers						
Number of red tiles	1	2	3	4	5	6
Number of white tiles		4				

C4 (a) Without drawing, how many white tiles would you need
for a tower that uses 8 red tiles?

(b) Check your result by drawing a tower that uses 8 red tiles.

C5 How many white tiles would you need for a tower with 15 red tiles?

C6 How many white tiles would you need for a tower with 40 red tiles?

C7 Explain how can you find the number of white tiles in a tower
if you know the number of red tiles.

C8 Work out how many white tiles you would need for a tower with

(a) 100 red tiles   (b) 58 red tiles

Tom calls these designs 'L-shapes'.

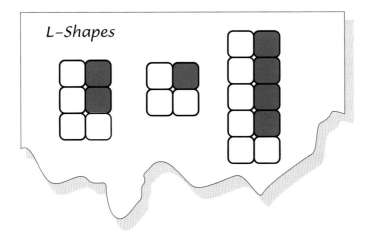

L–Shapes

C9 (a) Draw an L-shape that uses 5 red tiles.

(b) How many white tiles does it have?

C10 Copy and complete this table.

L-shapes						
Number of red tiles	1	2	3	4	5	6
Number of white tiles		4				

C11 (a) Without drawing, how many white tiles would you need for an L-shape that uses 9 red tiles?

(b) Check your result by drawing an L-shape that uses 9 red tiles.

C12 How many white tiles would you need for an L-shape with 26 red tiles?

C13 How many white tiles would you need for an L-shape with 100 red tiles?

C14 Explain how you can find the number of white tiles for an L-shape if you know number of red tiles.

D Bridges

Tom designs pieces for another mobile.
He calls them 'bridges'.

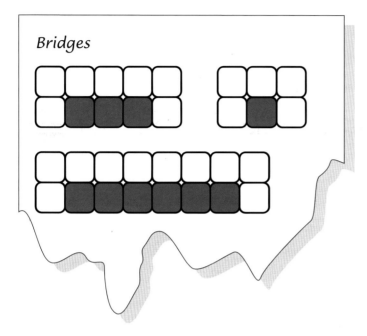

D1 How many white tiles are used for the piece with 6 red tiles?

D2 (a) Draw a bridge that uses 2 red tiles.

(b) How many white tiles does it have?

D3 (a) Draw a bridge with 4 red tiles.

(b) How many white tiles does it have?

D4 How many **red** tiles are used for a piece with 7 **white** tiles?

D5 Copy and complete this table.

Bridges						
Number of red tiles	1	2	3	4	5	6
Number of white tiles	5					

D6 (a) Without drawing, how many white tiles would you need for a bridge with 10 red tiles?

(b) Check your result by drawing a bridge with 10 red tiles.

D7 How many white tiles would you need for a bridge with 20 red tiles?

D8 How many white tiles would you need for a bridge with 50 red tiles?

D9

This bridge has 1000 red tiles! How many white tiles does it have?

D10 Explain how you can find the number of white tiles for a bridge if you know the number of red tiles.

D11 Work out how many white tiles you would need for a bridge with

(a) 25 red tiles   (b) 36 red tiles

▽■○ **D12** (a) Copy and complete this rule to give the link between the number of red tiles and the number of white tiles.

number of white tiles =

(b) Write out an explanation, like Sushma's or Tracy's on pages 116 and 117, saying why the rule works.

▽■○ **D13** Use the rule to work out how many white tiles you would need for a bridge with

(a) 83 red tiles   (b) 96 red tiles

▽■○ **D14** (a) How many **red** tiles would you need for a bridge with 52 **white** tiles?

(b) Explain how you worked out your answer.

E Surrounds

Tom calls these designs 'surrounds'.

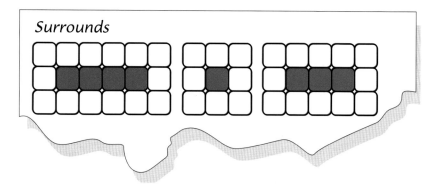

Surrounds

E1 (a) Draw a surround that uses 6 red tiles.

(b) How many white tiles does it have?

E2 Copy and complete this table.

Surrounds						
Number of red tiles	1	2	3	4	5	6
Number of white tiles			12			

E3 (a) Without drawing, how many red tiles would you need for a surround that uses 10 red tiles?

(b) Check your result by drawing a surround that uses 10 red tiles.

E4 How many white tiles would you need for a surround with 26 red tiles?

E5 How many white tiles would you need for a surround with 100 red tiles?

E6 Explain how you can find the number of white tiles for a surround if you know the number of red tiles.

▽■○ E7 (a) Copy and complete this rule to give the link between the number of red tiles and the number of white tiles.

> number of white tiles =

(b) Write out an explanation, like Sushma's or Tracy's on pages 116 and 117, saying why the rule works.

F More designs

F1 There are four sets of designs below.
For each set of designs,

   (a) find out how many white tiles you need for a piece
      with 100 red tiles

   (b) explain how you can find the number of white tiles
      if you know the number of red tiles

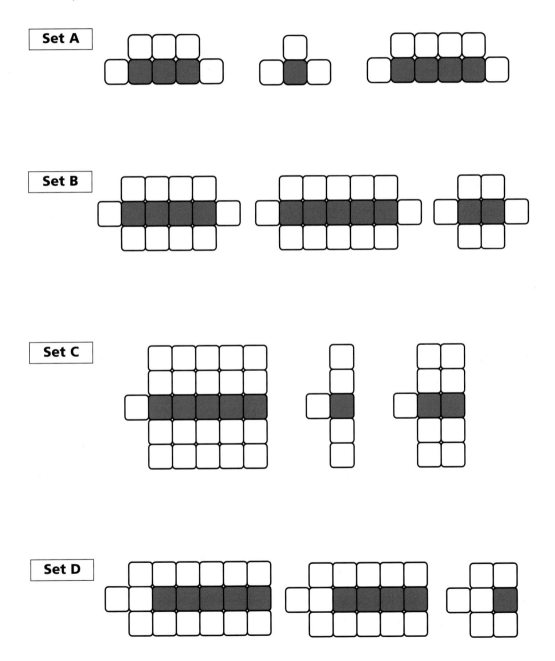

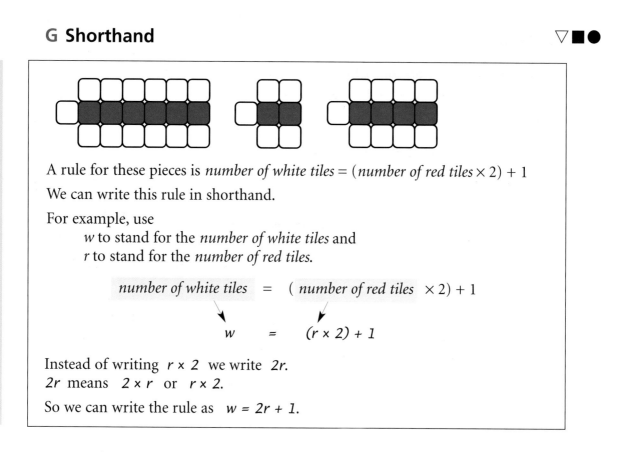

A rule for these pieces is *number of white tiles* = (*number of red tiles* × 2) + 1

We can write this rule in shorthand.

For example, use

w to stand for the *number of white tiles* and
r to stand for the *number of red tiles*.

$$number\ of\ white\ tiles\ =\ (\ number\ of\ red\ tiles\ \times 2) + 1$$

$$w\ =\ (r \times 2) + 1$$

Instead of writing *r × 2* we write *2r*.
2r means *2 × r* or *r × 2*.

So we can write the rule as *w = 2r + 1*.

G1 Sort these rules into four matching pairs.

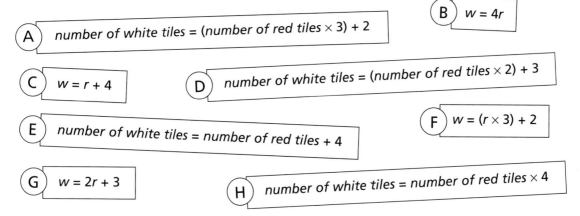

A) number of white tiles = (number of red tiles × 3) + 2

B) w = 4r

C) w = r + 4

D) number of white tiles = (number of red tiles × 2) + 3

E) number of white tiles = number of red tiles + 4

F) w = (r × 3) + 2

G) w = 2r + 3

H) number of white tiles = number of red tiles × 4

G2 Write each of these rules in shorthand.

(a) *number of white tiles* = (*number of red tiles* × 4) + 3

(b) *number of white tiles* = *number of red tiles* × 5

(c) *number of white tiles* = (*number of red tiles* × 2) + 7

(d) *number of white tiles* = *number of red tiles* + 6

(e) *number of white tiles* = (*number of red tiles* × 3) − 1

H Using shorthand

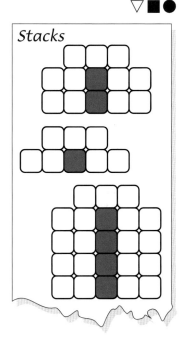

Stacks

H1 (a) Without drawing, how many white tiles would
you need for a stack that uses 5 red tiles?

(b) How can you check your result?

H2 How many white tiles would you need for a stack with

(a) 12 red tiles   (b) 60 red tiles

H3 (a) Copy and complete this rule to give the link
between the number of red tiles and the number
of white tiles.

> *number of white tiles =*

(b) Write your rule in shorthand.
Use *w* for the *number of white tiles*
and *r* for the *number of red tiles*.

(c) Explain how you found your rule.

H4 Use your rule to work out the number of white tiles
needed for a stack with

(a) 25 red tiles   (b) 40 red tiles

H5 (a) Design a set of pieces that fits the rule
$w = 2r + 2$

(b) Explain, using diagrams, how you know
your pieces fit the rule.

H6

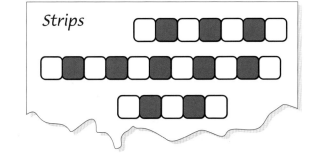

Strips

(a) For strips, find a rule that gives the link between
the number of red tiles and the number of white tiles.

(b) Explain how you found your rule.

H7 Find a rule for each set of pieces below.
Explain how you found each rule.

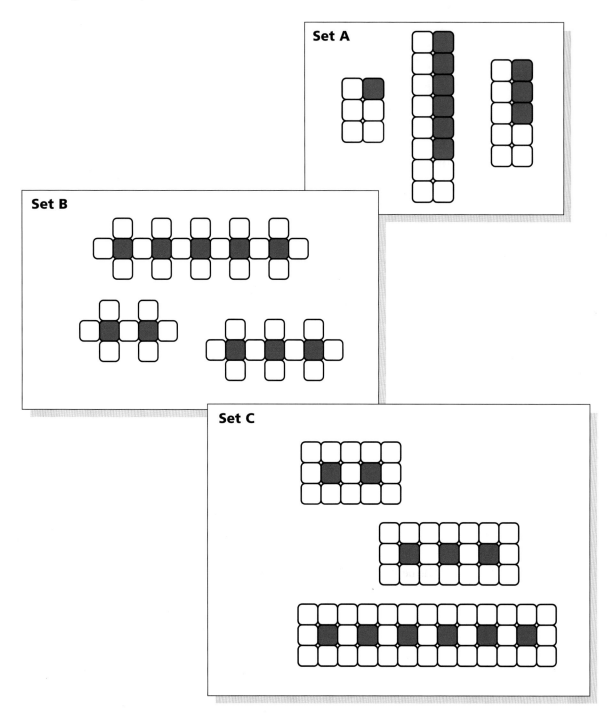

I T-shapes and more

▽ □ ●

Pieces like this are called 'T-shapes'.

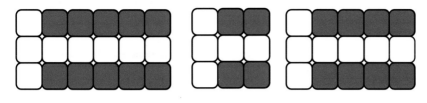

Jan found a rule for T-shapes like this.

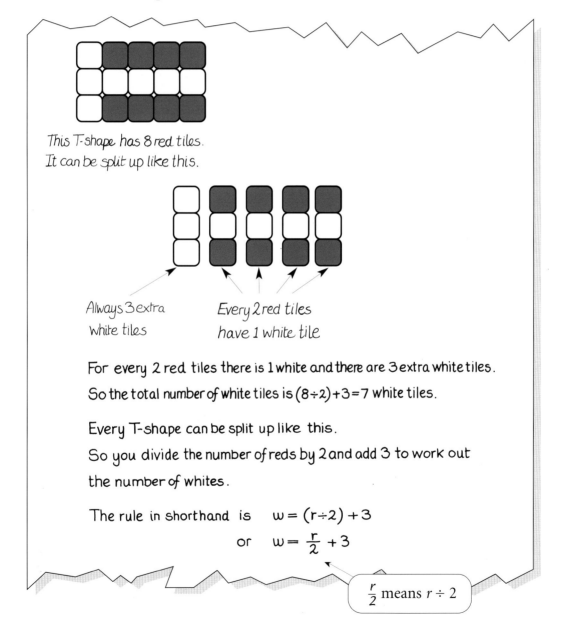

This T-shape has 8 red tiles.
It can be split up like this.

Always 3 extra
white tiles

Every 2 red tiles
have 1 white tile

For every 2 red tiles there is 1 white and there are 3 extra white tiles.
So the total number of white tiles is $(8 \div 2) + 3 = 7$ white tiles.

Every T-shape can be split up like this.
So you divide the number of reds by 2 and add 3 to work out the number of whites.

The rule in shorthand is $\quad w = (r \div 2) + 3$

$\qquad$ or $\quad w = \dfrac{r}{2} + 3$

$\dfrac{r}{2}$ means $r \div 2$

I1 For each set of pieces

    (a) find a rule in the form '$w = \ldots$'

    (b) explain how you found the rule

    (c) use your rule to find the number of white tiles
        needed for a piece with 100 red tiles

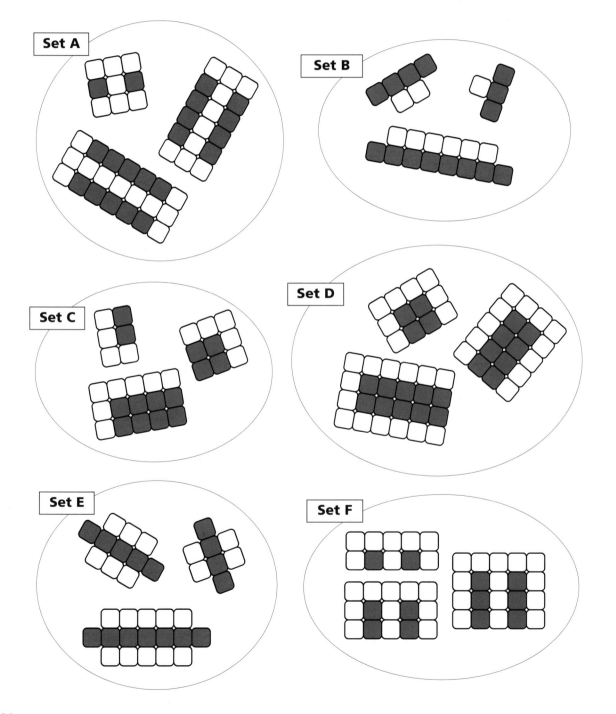

J Snails and hats

Julie calls pieces like this 'snails'.

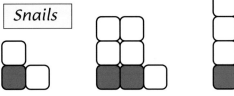

J1 How many white tiles are used for the snail with 3 red tiles?

J2 (a) Draw a snail that uses 4 red tiles.

(b) How many white tiles does it have?

J3 Without drawing, how many white tiles would you need
for a snail that uses 6 red tiles?

J4 How many white tiles would you need for a snail
that uses 10 red tiles?

J5 How many white tiles are needed for a snail that uses 20 reds?

J6 Explain how to find the number of white tiles in a snail
if you know the number of red tiles.

J7 Copy and complete this table.

Snails						
Number of red tiles	1	2	3	4	5	6
Number of white tiles		5				

J8 (a) Describe how the number of white tiles goes up
as the number of red tiles goes up.

(b) Try to explain why the number of white tiles
goes up in this way.

J9 (a) How many white tiles would you need for a snail
that uses 7 red tiles?

(b) Explain how you worked out your answer.

J10 Julie makes a snail that uses 145 **white** tiles.
How many **red** tiles did she use?

Steve calls these pieces 'hats'.

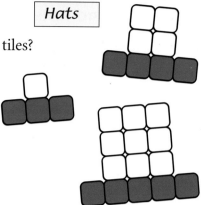

Hats

J11 How many white tiles are used for the hat with 4 red tiles?

J12 (a) Draw a hat that uses 6 red tiles.

(b) How many white tiles does it have?

J13 How many white tiles would you need for a hat that uses 12 red tiles?

J14 Explain how you can find the number of white tiles in a hat if you know the number of red tiles.

J15 How many white tiles would you need for a hat that uses 25 red tiles?

J16 Steve makes a hat that uses 64 white tiles. How many red tiles did he use?

J17 Explain why it is impossible to make a hat with 200 white tiles.

*__J18__ This question is on sheet 89.

What progress have you made?

Statement

▼■● I can find and use rules,
↓   describing them in words.

Evidence

These pieces are called 'drops'.

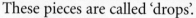

Drops

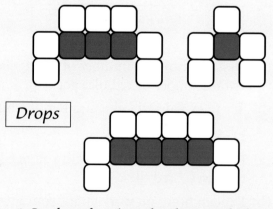

1 Look at the piece that has 4 red tiles. How many white tiles does it have?

2 (a) Draw the piece that uses 5 red tiles.

(b) How many white tiles does it use?

I can find and use rules, describing them in words.

3 Copy and complete this table for the drops.

Number of red tiles	1	2	3	4	5
Number of white tiles			7		

4 How many white tiles would you need for a piece with

(a) 7 red tiles   (b) 10 red tiles

5 How many white tiles would you need for a piece with 100 red tiles?

6 Explain how you can work out the number of white tiles if you know the number of red tiles.

Here are some pieces from another mobile.

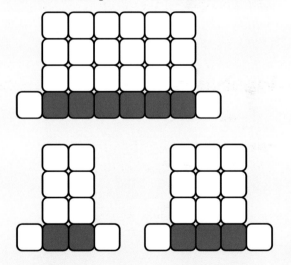

7 Without drawing, how many white tiles would you need for a piece that uses 5 red tiles?

8 How many white tiles would you need for a piece with 100 red tiles?

9 Explain how you can work out the number of white tiles if you know the number of red tiles.

Statement	**Evidence**

▽■●
↓   I can understand and use algebraic shorthand.

10 A rule for a set of mobile pieces is
$$w = 5r + 3$$

w stands for the number of white tiles.
r stands for the number of red tiles.

Use the rule to find the number of white tiles needed for a piece with 6 red tiles.

11 Write each of the rules below in shorthand. Use w to stand for the number of white tiles and r to stand for the number of red tiles.

(a) *number of white tiles =*
    number of red tiles + 8

(b) *number of white tiles =*
    (number of red tiles × 4) + 1

I can find and use rules, describing them in shorthand.

12 For the set of pieces below

(a) find a rule in the form $w = \ldots$

(b) explain how you found the rule

(c) use the rule to find how many white tiles are needed for a piece with 50 red tiles

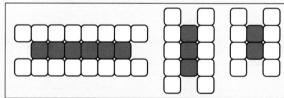

▽□●
I can find and use more complex rules, describing them in shorthand.

13 For each set of pieces below

(a) find a rule in the form $w = \ldots$

(b) explain how you found your rule

(c) use your rule to work out how many white tiles are needed for a piece with 100 reds

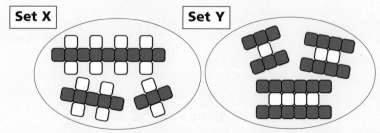

Set X   Set Y

Area and perimeter

This work will help you

◆ work out the perimeter of a simple shape

◆ work out an area in square centimetres (cm²) or square metres (m²)

◆ work out a shape's area by splitting it into simpler shapes

◆ solve problems involving areas and perimeters

A Exploring perimeters ▼■●

Work on centimetre squared paper for these investigations.

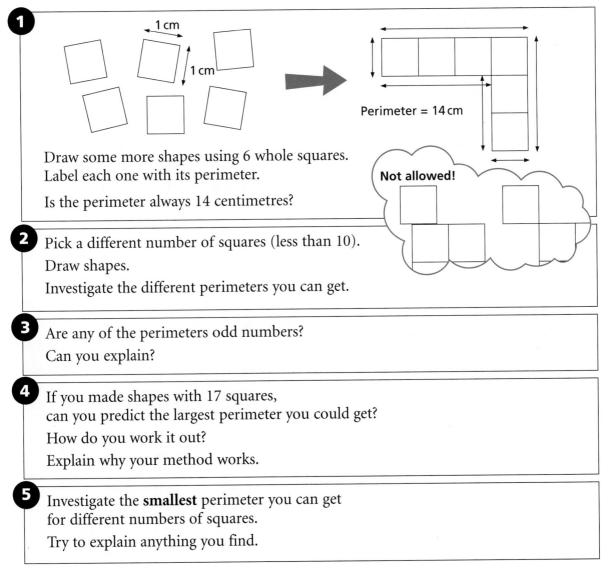

1 Draw some more shapes using 6 whole squares.
Label each one with its perimeter.

Is the perimeter always 14 centimetres?

Not allowed!

Perimeter = 14 cm

2 Pick a different number of squares (less than 10).
Draw shapes.
Investigate the different perimeters you can get.

3 Are any of the perimeters odd numbers?
Can you explain?

4 If you made shapes with 17 squares,
can you predict the largest perimeter you could get?
How do you work it out?
Explain why your method works.

5 Investigate the **smallest** perimeter you can get
for different numbers of squares.
Try to explain anything you find.

B Square centimetres

The **area** of one square on this grid
is **1 square centimetre.**

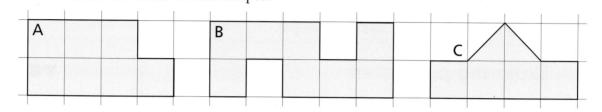

We write **1 cm²** for short.

B1 What are the areas of these shapes?

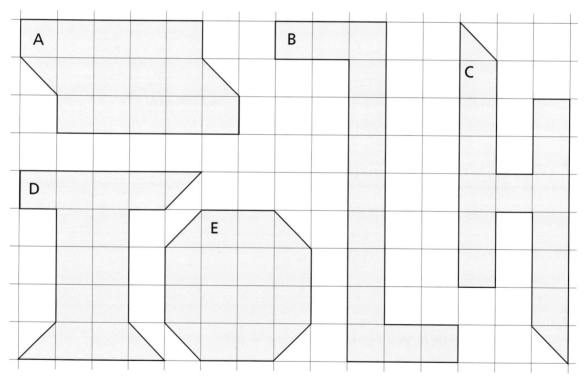

B2 (a) Which of these shapes has the largest area?

(b) Which has the smallest area?

(c) Do any of them have the same area?

B3 On centimetre squared paper draw three shapes with
areas that are nearly the same but not quite the same.

Give your shapes to a partner.
Challenge them to say which has the largest area just by looking.
Then they can check to see if they were right.

C The area of a rectangle

▼■○

C1 What is the area of this rectangle in cm²?
Draw some other rectangles with the same area.

C2 Find three rectangles with an area of 40 cm².
Write down the length and width of each one.

C3 How many rectangles can you find with an area of 16 cm²?
Write down the length and width of each one.

C4 Find the areas of these rectangles.

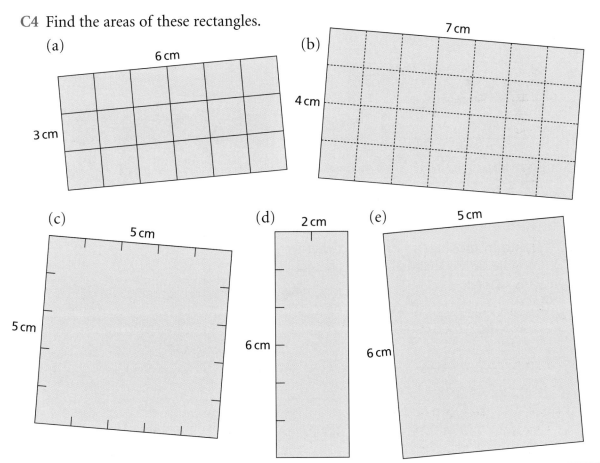

(a) 6 cm, 3 cm

(b) 7 cm, 4 cm

(c) 5 cm, 5 cm

(d) 2 cm, 6 cm

(e) 5 cm, 6 cm

D Measuring to find areas

D1 A printer makes a set of gift tags.
Measure to find the area of each tag.

(a)

(b)

(c)

(d)

(e)

(f) 140°

(g)

(h)

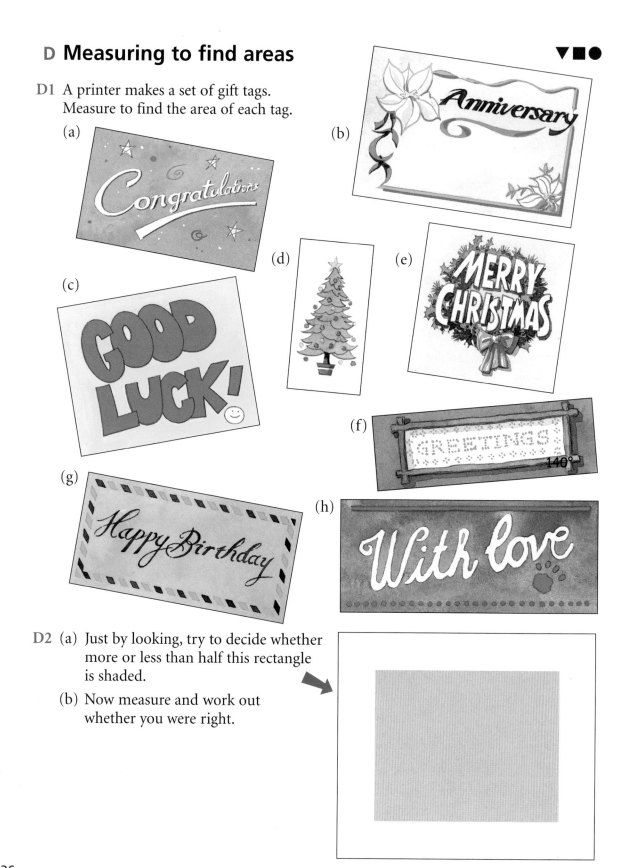

D2 (a) Just by looking, try to decide whether
more or less than half this rectangle
is shaded.

    (b) Now measure and work out
whether you were right.

D3 Find the missing length for each rectangle.
(These are sketches, not accurate drawings.)

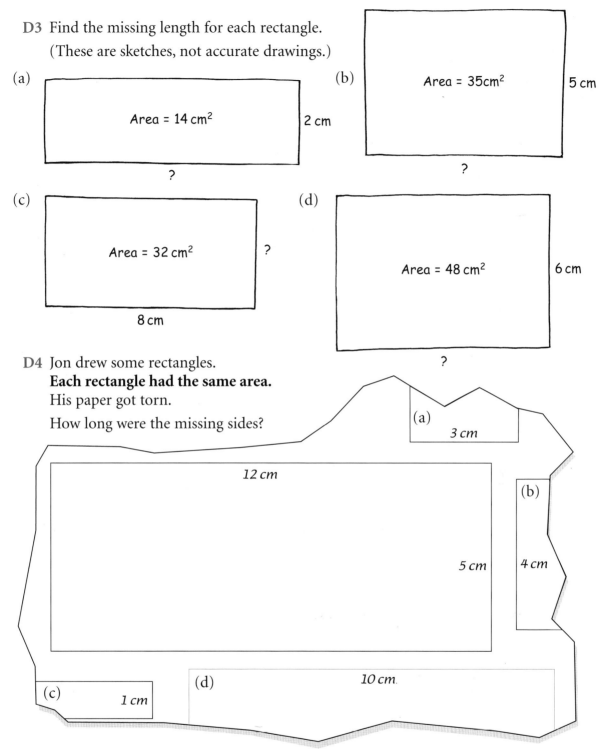

(a) Area = 14 cm²   2 cm   ?

(b) Area = 35cm²   5 cm   ?

(c) Area = 32 cm²   ?   8 cm

(d) Area = 48 cm²   6 cm   ?

D4 Jon drew some rectangles.
Each rectangle had the same area.
His paper got torn.

How long were the missing sides?

(a) 3 cm

12 cm

(b)

5 cm   4 cm

(c) 1 cm

(d) 10 cm

D5 The corners of a rectangle have these coordinates:
(0, 4), (9, 4), (9, 1), (0, 1)

Draw the rectangle on centimetre squared paper.
Find its area.

E It pays to advertise

E1 The Timesham *Weekly News* charges £1 per cm² for adverts.

How much will each of these cost?
(Write down your measurements each time.)

(a) **Fiona's Flowers**

"They're blooming marvellous!!"
21 High St., Timesham

(b) **Summer Bonanza**

Pine shelves £99
Bookshelves £89
Pine beds £199
Tables £129

THE PINE PLACE

(c) **Mary's Cattery**

The "Purrfect" home from home for your cat
Tel: Timesham 987654

(d) **Chequers**
Night Club

Why not check us out!

Fridays, The Brewhouse
Old Market St. 11 – 3am

(e) **R G SPARK & SON**

ELECTRICAL CONTRACTORS
& ENGINEERS

COMMERCIAL•INDUSTRIAL
• RETAIL

Installers of:
• Lighting
• Alarms
• Cabling
• Inspection & Testing

Unit 4, Timesham Business Park   Tel: 123467

(f) **MARTINS**
of Timesham

ANNISSA

SERVICING
SALES
MOT

OPEN SEVEN DAYS
A WEEK

Otherplace Rd
opposite "The Sun"

E2 The Timesham *Evening Echo* has more readers.
So it can charge £2 per cm² for adverts.

How much will each of these cost?
(Write down your measurements.)

(a)

GARDEN SUPPLIES

Specialists in Garden Furniture
Many styles of Tables and chairs,
Pergolas, Fencing etc.

Timesham 123578

(b)

B. F. Pie

Quality
Butcher

Prizewinning game sausages

Free Local delivery

14 Lamb St., Lower Timesham
Telephone: 876543

(c)

THE SUN INN   Tel: 124689

Fine Pub Food
A selection of Real Ales
Traditional games
A la carte restaurant and function room

(d)
Plumbing problem?
Call Lee King
for emergency service
24 hrs Mobile 0808 888222

(e)

Family business
established over
100 years

RUDYARDS

Bakers of Timesham

Celebration cakes
Pastries &
Freshly baked bread

18 High St. Timesham   126543

(f)

Diana's
Mobile hairdressing

TELEPHONE: 777 242424

✂ D. Salon MPHA

F Square metres ▼■●

The areas of floors, walls, gardens and so on are measured in square metres (m² for short). Square centimetres are too small.

Estimate these in square metres:

- the area of your classroom floor
- the area of one of the walls

Now measure to see how close you were.

F1 Find the area of the whole of this floor in square metres.

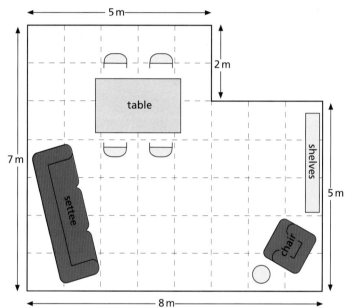

You can find the area of some 'awkward' shapes by splitting them into rectangles.

For example, this L-shape can be split into two rectangles A and B.

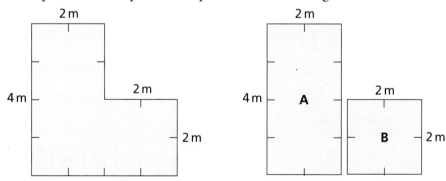

F2 (a) What is the area of rectangle A?

(b) What is the area of rectangle B?

(c) What is the area of the whole L-shape?

F3 Draw a sketch of this L-shape.
Split it into rectangles.
Work out the area of the whole shape.

Now split it a different way to
work out the area of the whole shape.

Check that both ways give you the same area.

F4 **Work with a partner.**
Work out the area of each of the shapes below.
You split up each shape one way, and your partner in another way.

Check you both get the same answers.

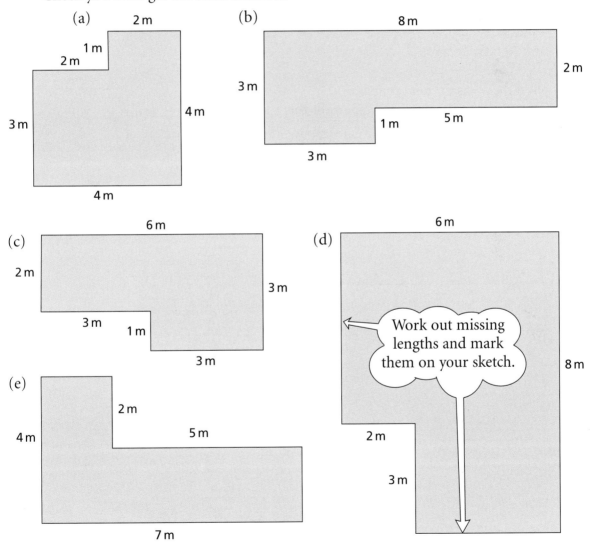

F5 Work out the perimeters of the shapes in question F4.

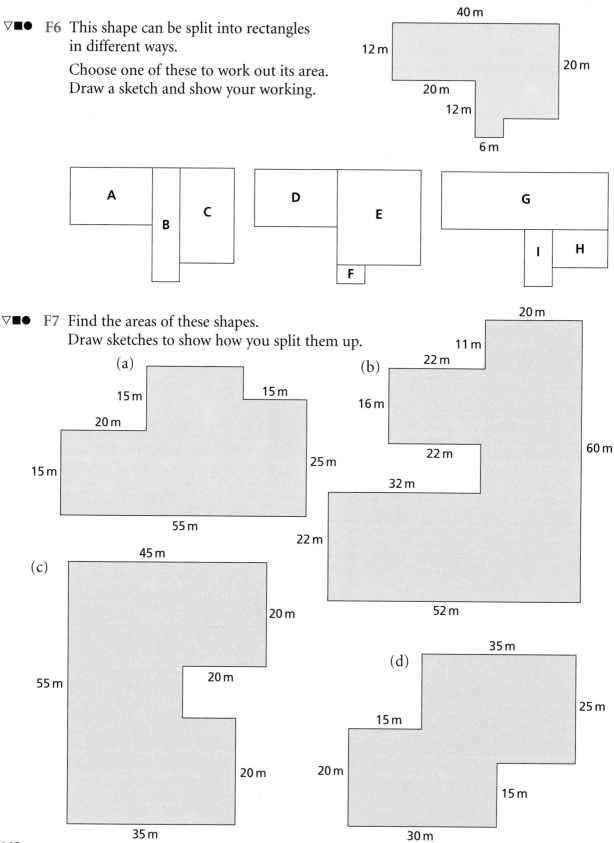

▽■● **F6** This shape can be split into rectangles in different ways.

Choose one of these to work out its area. Draw a sketch and show your working.

40 m
12 m
20 m
20 m
12 m
6 m

A
B
C

D
E
F

G
I
H

▽■● **F7** Find the areas of these shapes.
Draw sketches to show how you split them up.

(a)
15 m
15 m
20 m
25 m
15 m
55 m

(b)
20 m
11 m
22 m
16 m
22 m
32 m
60 m
22 m
52 m

(c)
45 m
20 m
55 m
20 m
20 m
35 m

(d)
35 m
25 m
15 m
20 m
20 m
15 m
30 m

▽■● **F8** You can think of this shape as rectangle A with rectangles B and C removed.

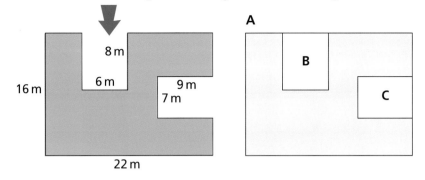

Work out the areas of rectangles A, B and C.

Subtract to find the area of the dark shape.

▽■● **F9** Find the area of these shapes by subtraction.

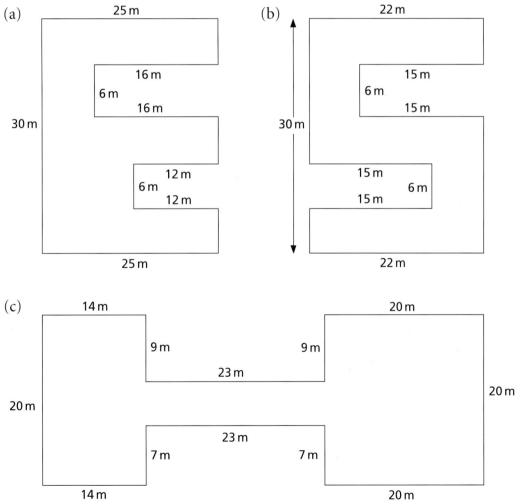

G Bringing in triangles

▽■●

G1 (a) What fraction of this rectangle is coloured blue?

   (b) What is the area of the blue triangle?

G2 What is the area of each triangle?

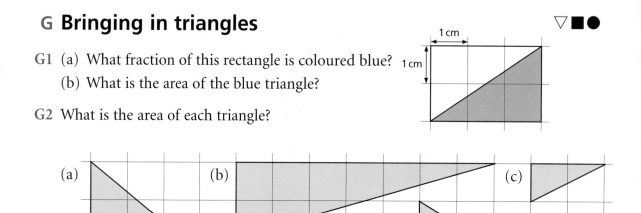

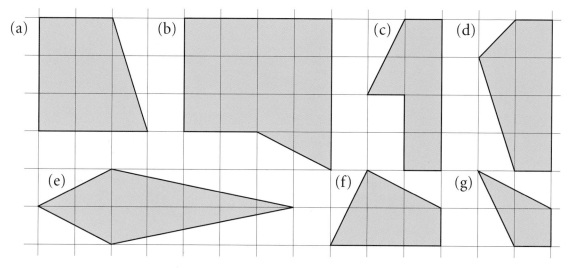

G3 What is the area of each shape?

G4 What is the area of each shape?

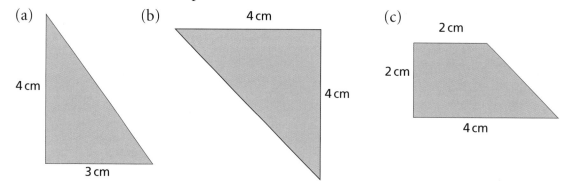

(a) 4 cm, 3 cm

(b) 4 cm, 4 cm

(c) 2 cm, 2 cm, 4 cm

H Using decimals

H1 Find the areas of these rectangles by
counting squares and fractions of squares.

Write any fractions in your answers as decimals.

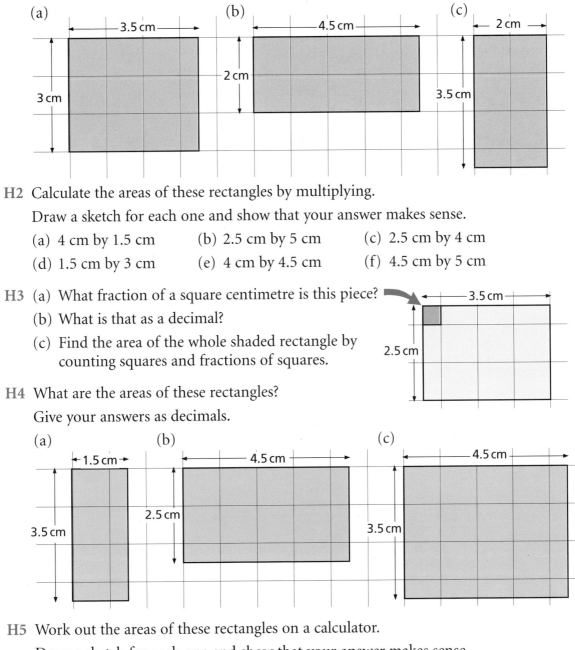

(a)
3.5 cm
3 cm

(b)
4.5 cm
2 cm

(c)
2 cm
3.5 cm

H2 Calculate the areas of these rectangles by multiplying.

Draw a sketch for each one and show that your answer makes sense.

(a) 4 cm by 1.5 cm   (b) 2.5 cm by 5 cm   (c) 2.5 cm by 4 cm

(d) 1.5 cm by 3 cm   (e) 4 cm by 4.5 cm   (f) 4.5 cm by 5 cm

H3 (a) What fraction of a square centimetre is this piece?

     (b) What is that as a decimal?

     (c) Find the area of the whole shaded rectangle by
        counting squares and fractions of squares.

3.5 cm
2.5 cm

H4 What are the areas of these rectangles?

Give your answers as decimals.

(a)
1.5 cm
3.5 cm

(b)
4.5 cm
2.5 cm

(c)
4.5 cm
3.5 cm

H5 Work out the areas of these rectangles on a calculator.

Draw a sketch for each one and show that your answer makes sense.

(a) 2.5 cm by 1.5 cm   (b) 5.5 cm by 2.5 cm   (c) 3.5 cm by 6.5 cm

(d) 1.5 cm by 0.5 cm   (e) 2.5 cm by 2.5 cm   (f) 1.5 cm by 5.5 cm

H6 Sheena drew six rectangles all with the same area.
She spilt ink on her paper.

How long were the hidden sides?

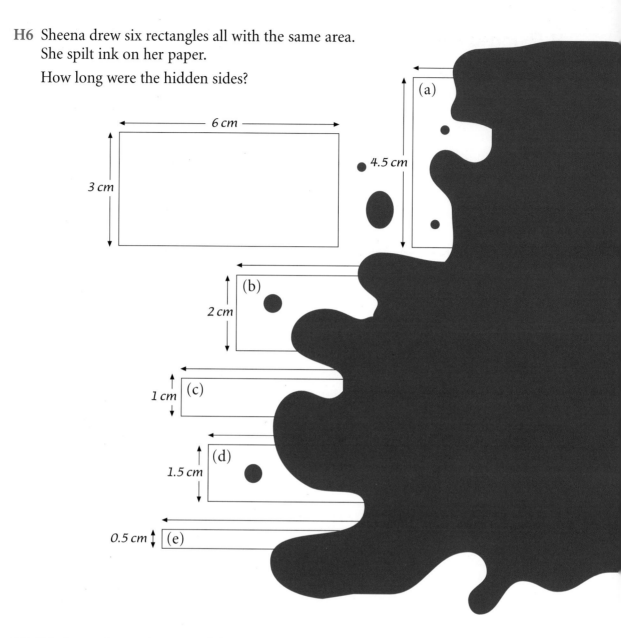

H7 Work out the perimeters of the rectangles in question H2.

H8 Work out the perimeters of the rectangles in question H5.

▽□● **H9** Work out the length and width of rectangles with
   (a) area 4.5 cm² and perimeter 9 cm
   (b) area 5 cm² and perimeter 9 cm
   (c) area 10 cm² and perimeter 13 cm
   (d) area 19.25 cm² and perimeter 18 cm

I Further decimals

If you divide a square metre into ten equal parts, each part is 0.1 m².

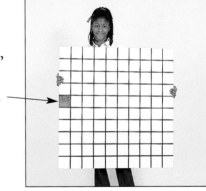

I1 Write each of the areas coloured red as decimals of a square metre.

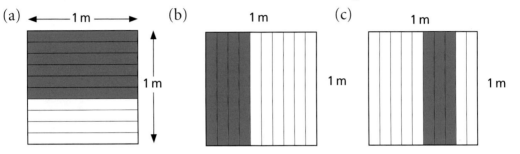

(a)   1 m   1 m
(b)   1 m   1 m
(c)   1 m   1 m

If you divide a square metre into squares 0.1 m by 0.1 m, you get 100 of them.

So each small square is $\frac{1}{100}$ of a square metre, or 0.01 m².

I2 Write each area coloured red as a decimal of a square metre.

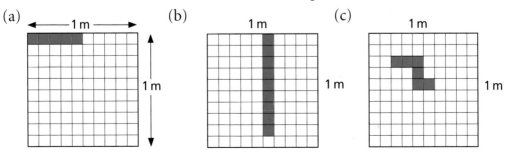

(a)   1 m   1 m
(b)   1 m   1 m
(c)   1 m   1 m

147

3 tenths of a square metre and 4 hundredths
have been coloured red here.

So 0.34 m² is red.

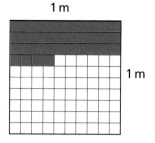

I3 Write these red areas as decimals of a square metre.

(a) 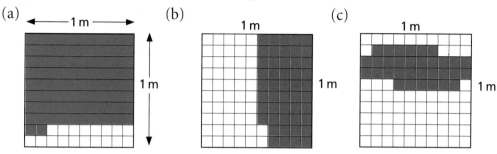 (b)   (c)

I4 This doormat has been placed on a metre square.

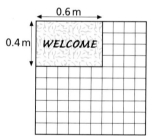

(a) How many hundredths of a square metre
does the doormat cover?

(b) What is that as a decimal?

(c) Work out the area of the doormat on your calculator.
If you don't get the same answer as (b),
try to find out why.

I5 For each of these doormats

(a) write how many hundredths of a square metre it covers

(b) give this as a decimal

(c) check with a calculator

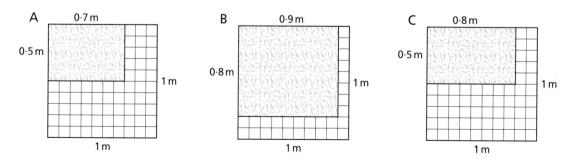

I6 Work out the areas of these rectangles.

(a) 0.6 m by 0.3 m   (b) 0.7 m by 0.6 m   (c) 0.5 m by 0.2 m

I7 Emma says:

> 0.4 × 0.2 = 0.8

Is she right?

Use a diagram like those on the opposite page to explain.

I8 Work out the areas of these rectangles.

(a) 0.3 m by 0.2 m   (b) 0.5 m by 0.1 m   (c) 0.4 m by 0.3 m

(d) 0.4 m by 0.5 m   (e) 0.5 m by 0.8 m   (f) 0.5 m by 1.0 m

This doormat is a rectangle 0.8 m by 2.0 m.

The doormat has been placed on two square metre grids.
Each square on the grids is one hundredth of a square metre.

I9 (a) How many hundredths of a square metre does the doormat cover?

(b) What is that as a decimal?

(c) Check with a calculator.

I10 Work out the areas of these doormats.

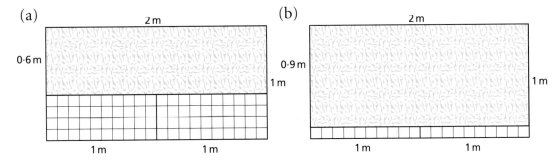

(a) 2 m, 0.6 m, 1 m, 1 m, 1 m

(b) 2 m, 0.9 m, 1 m, 1 m, 1 m, 1 m

149

The Ritz Hotel's big doormat

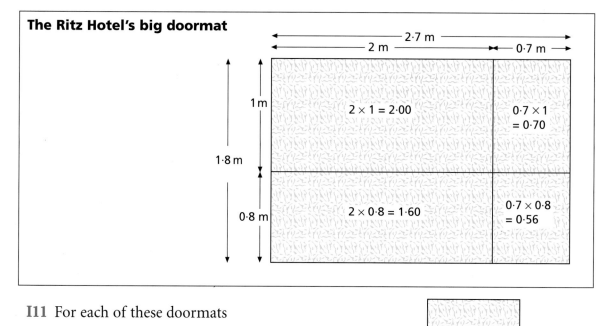

I11 For each of these doormats

    (a) draw a sketch dividing it up as for the Ritz Hotel

    (b) write an area calculation in each section

    (c) work out the total of these areas

    (d) check by multiplying the length and width
        of the whole doormat on a calculator

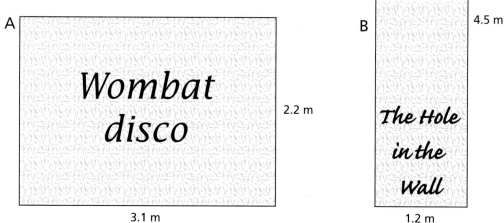

A

Wombat disco

2.2 m

3.1 m

B

The Hole in the Wall

4.5 m

1.2 m

C

Marks and Spencer's

1.4 m

6.2 m

I12 Work out the areas of these rectangles.

(a) 4.1 cm / 2.8 cm

(b) 3.2 cm / 2.5 cm

(c) 4.5 cm / 3.6 cm

I13 The Timesham *Weekly News* charges £1 per cm² for adverts.

How much will each of these cost?
(Write down your measurements each time.)

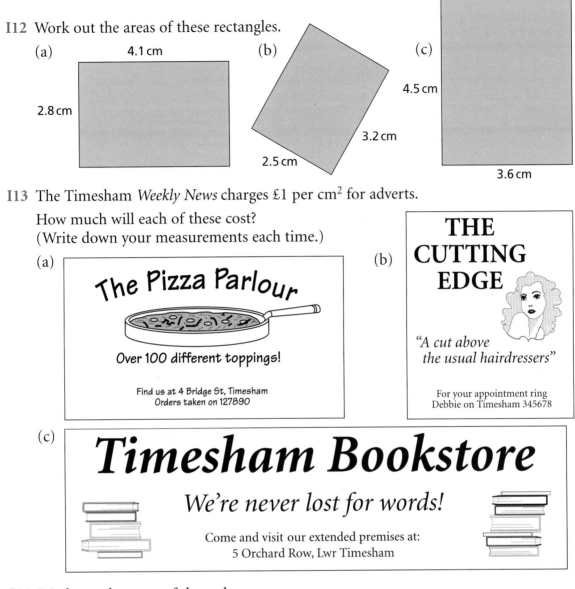

(a) **The Pizza Parlour**
Over 100 different toppings!
Find us at 4 Bridge St, Timesham
Orders taken on 127890

(b) **THE CUTTING EDGE**
"A cut above the usual hairdressers"
For your appointment ring
Debbie on Timesham 345678

(c) **Timesham Bookstore**
We're never lost for words!
Come and visit our extended premises at:
5 Orchard Row, Lwr Timesham

I14 Work out the areas of these shapes.

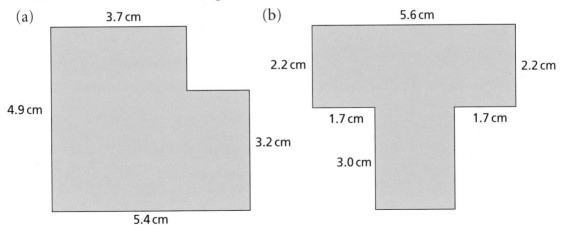

(a) 3.7 cm / 4.9 cm / 3.2 cm / 5.4 cm

(b) 5.6 cm / 2.2 cm / 2.2 cm / 1.7 cm / 1.7 cm / 3.0 cm

I15 Find the missing length in each of these.

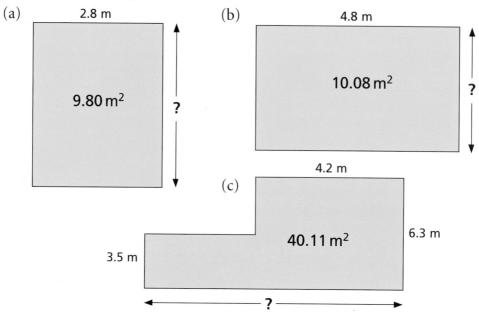

(a) 2.8 m — 9.80 m² — ?

(b) 4.8 m — 10.08 m² — ?

(c) 4.2 m — 40.11 m² — 6.3 m — 3.5 m — ?

I16 A rectangle's area is 36.00 cm² and its perimeter is 24.6 cm.
What are its length and width?

I17 What is the area of each triangle?

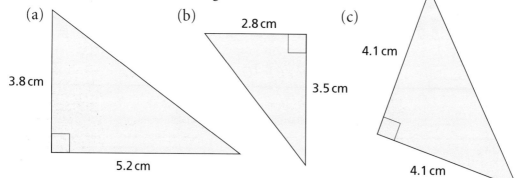

(a) 3.8 cm — 5.2 cm

(b) 2.8 cm — 3.5 cm

(c) 4.1 cm — 4.1 cm

I18 What is the area of each of these shapes?
Draw a sketch of each one to show how you split it up.

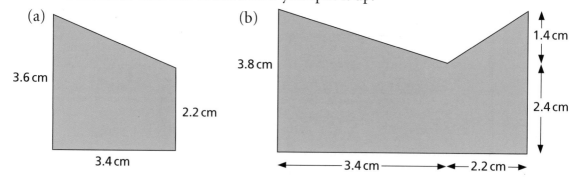

(a) 3.6 cm — 2.2 cm — 3.4 cm

(b) 3.8 cm — 1.4 cm — 2.4 cm — 3.4 cm — 2.2 cm

152

I19 A jeweller has designed these earrings.
To find the amount of metal used for each one,

- make a sketch
- take the measurements you need and
  mark them on your sketch
- work out the total area

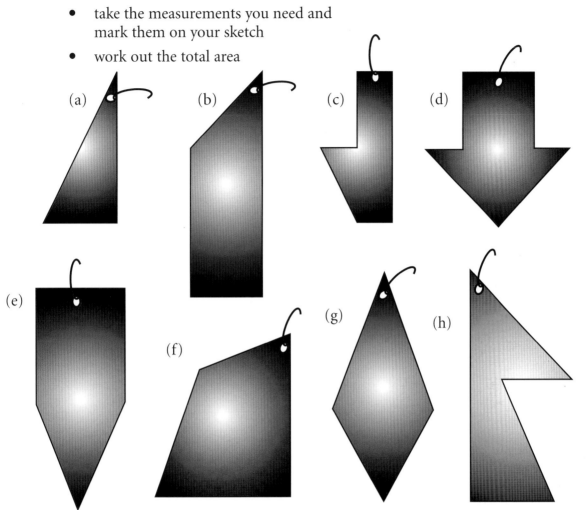

(a) (b) (c) (d) (e) (f) (g) (h)

Design some earrings of your own like these.
Find their area.

True or false?

- You can't talk about the area of England,
  because it doesn't have straight sides.

- You can't talk about the area of an animal's skin,
  because it isn't flat.

- A map of the world is useful for comparing
  the areas of different countries.

Safely grazing ▼■●

An investigation

A shepherdess wants to make a pen for her sheep.
She only has 40 m of fencing.

This is one possible pen
she could make.

What is the area of this pen?

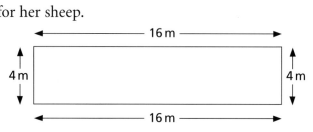

Draw some other rectangular pens she could make using all her fencing.
Find the areas of these pens.

What length and width give the biggest area of pen?

Try with some other lengths of fencing.
Draw some sketches and write about your findings.

What progress have you made?

Statement

▼■●
↓   I can find the area and
perimeter of a rectangle.

I can find areas and perimeters
of shapes by splitting them up.

Evidence

1 Measure this label.
Work out its area and perimeter.

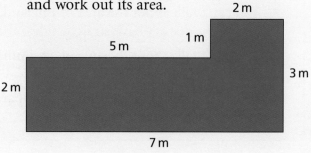

2 Draw a sketch of this L-shape.
Split it into rectangles
and work out its area.

Statement	Evidence

▽■● I can find areas and perimeters
↓ of rectangles involving simple
decimals.

3 What is the area and perimeter of
each of these rectangles?
Give your answers as decimals.

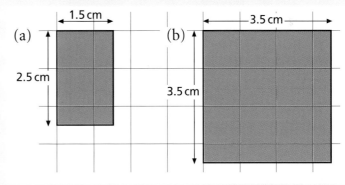

(a) 1.5 cm 2.5 cm

(b) 3.5 cm 3.5 cm

I can find areas of shapes with
triangles in them.

4 What is the area of each of these shapes?

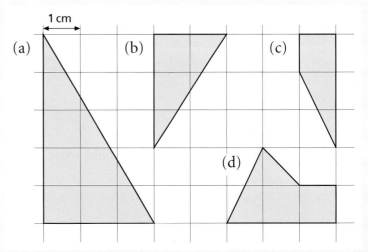

1 cm

(a) (b) (c) (d)

▽□●
I can find areas of
rectangles involving
more complex
decimals.

5 Work out the area of each of these rectangles.

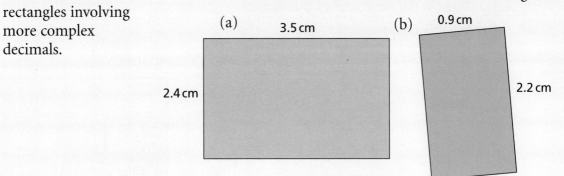

(a) 3.5 cm 2.4 cm

(b) 0.9 cm 2.2 cm

Review 3

▼□○ **1** Write down the coordinates of
↓ each corner of this shape.

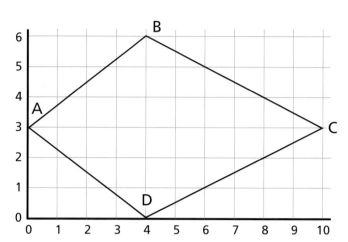

2 Work out the weight of a bottle.

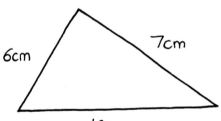

3 Draw this triangle accurately.
You need a ruler and a pencil, but what else?

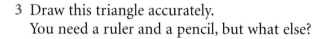

6cm   7cm

10cm

4 (a) What is the perimeter of this shape?
(b) What is the area of the shape?

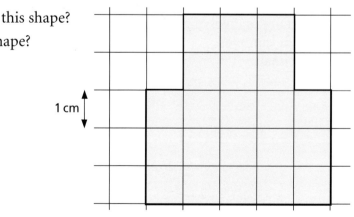

1 cm

5 Draw an angle of 30°.

Mark a point 8 cm along each 'arm', like this.

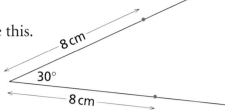

Join the two points with a straight line.
Measure the line and write down its length.

6 Here are some tile patterns.

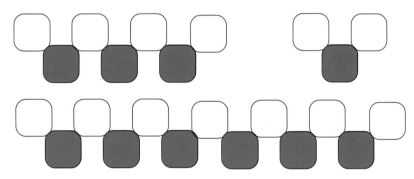

(a) Draw the pattern that has 4 red tiles.
How many white tiles does it have?

(b) Copy and complete this table.

Number of red tiles	1	2	3	4	5	6	7
Number of white tiles			4				

(c) How many white tiles would you need for a pattern with
(i) 10 red tiles   (ii) 50 red tiles

(d) Explain how you worked out your answers to (c).

(e) How can you work out the number of white tiles
if you know the number of red tiles?

▽■○ **7** Work out the angles marked with letters.
↓

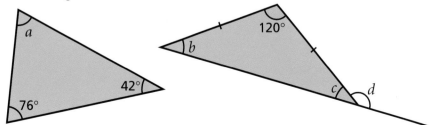

157

8 Work out the missing numbers.

(a) $12 - (\boxed{} + 4) = 2$ (b) $24 \div (2 \times \boxed{}) = 3$ (c) $18 - (7 - \boxed{}) = 13$

9

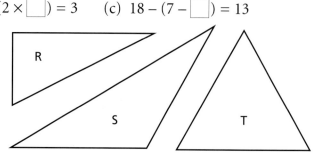

Which of these triangles is

(a) equilateral (b) isosceles and right-angled

(c) isosceles and not right-angled (d) right-angled and scalene

(e) scalene and not right-angled

10 Work out the weight of a bottle.

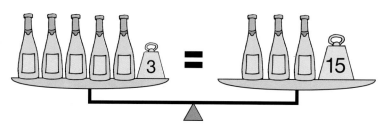

11 Here are some tile patterns.

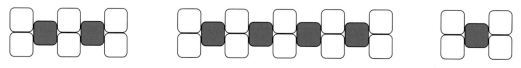

Find a rule connecting the number of red tiles and the number of white tiles.
Use r for the number of red tiles and w for the number of white tiles.

12 Find the area of each of these shapes.

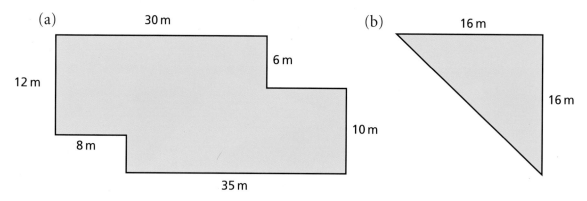

(a) 30 m 12 m 6 m 8 m 35 m 10 m

(b) 16 m 16 m

▽□● 13 Calculate the angles marked with letters.

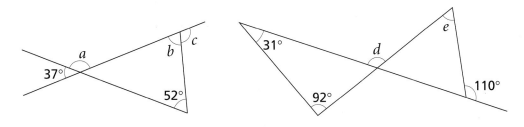

14 Find a rule connecting the numbers of red and white tiles in patterns like these.

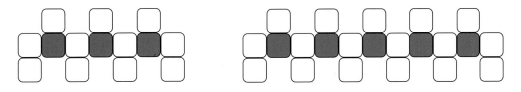

15 Find the lengths marked with letters.

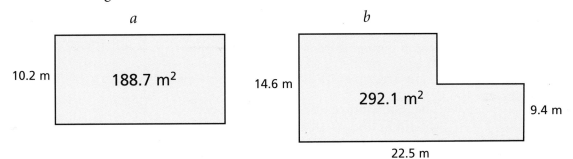

16 Solve these puzzles.

  (a) $4u + 7 = u + 19$ (b) $26 + 2v = 7v + 11$ (c) $3w + 14 = 5w + 9$

17 There are three isosceles triangles in this diagram.
   Lines with the same markings are the same length.

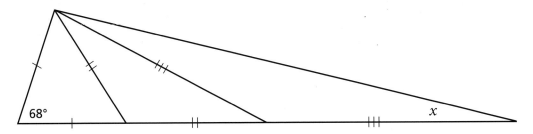

Calculate the angle marked x. Show how you worked it out.

⑭ Negative numbers

This work will help you

◆ understand negative numbers in temperatures

◆ read graphs involving negative temperatures

◆ work out temperature changes and do other calculations with negative numbers

A Colder and colder   ▼■●

Temperature is usually measured in **degrees Celsius** (°C).

Water boils at 100°C.

Room temperature is about 20°C.

Water freezes at 0°C.

The temperature inside a home freezer should be about ⁻18°C.

Temp °C
40
39
38
37
36
35
34
33
32
31
30
29
28
27
26
25
24
23
22
21
20
19
18
17
16
15
14
13
12
11
10
9
8
7
6
5
4
3
2
1
0
⁻1
⁻2
⁻3
⁻4
⁻5
⁻6
⁻7
⁻8
⁻9
⁻10
⁻11
⁻12
⁻13
⁻14
⁻15
⁻16
⁻17
⁻18
⁻19
⁻20

What kinds of thermometer have you seen?

For discussion

Put these temperatures in order from the highest to the lowest.

A A winter's day temperature at the North Pole

B Human body temperature

C Temperature of a hot summer's day in Britain

D Antarctic sea water temperature

E Temperature inside an ordinary fridge

F Temperature inside a car in the morning after a frosty night

G Temperature of a hot bath

H Temperature at which butter melts

I Temperature of a hot bowl of soup

J Oven temperature for baking a cake

K Temperature of ice-cream when it's good to eat

L Temperature of a heated swimming pool

A1 This question is on sheet 90.

A2 (a) What temperature is 5 degrees lower than 20°C?

(b) What temperature is 5 degrees higher than 20°C?

(c) Which is the colder temperature, ⁻1°C or ⁻2°C?

A3 (a) Which of these temperatures is lowest?

⁻6°C ⁻4°C ⁻8°C

(b) Which of these temperatures is highest?

⁻10°C ⁻2°C ⁻3°C

(c) Which of these temperatures is highest?

⁻10°C 2°C ⁻6°C

(d) Which of these temperatures is lowest?

7°C ⁻9°C ⁻4°C

A4 (a) What temperature is 5 degrees higher than 2°C?

(b) What temperature is 3 degrees lower than 2°C?

(c) What temperature is 3 degrees lower than ⁻2°C?

(d) What temperature is 30 degrees lower than ⁻20°C?

A5 Make some true sentences by putting any of the numbers below in the spaces.

A temperature of ....°C is ...... degrees higher than a temperature of ....°C.

⁻10	⁻5	0

5	10	15

A6 Make some true sentences by putting any of the numbers above into the spaces.

A temperature of ....°C is ...... degrees lower than a temperature of ....°C.

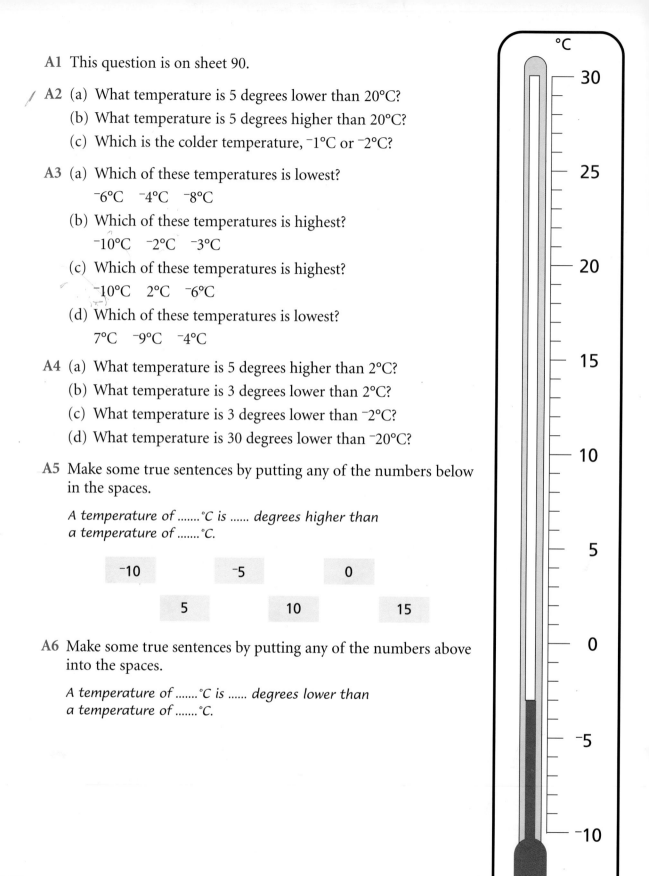

▽■● **A7** This table shows the average monthly temperatures
at Scott base (in Antarctica) and Nord base (in the Arctic).

Month	Jan	Feb	Mar	Apr	May	Jun	Jul	Aug	Sep	Oct	Nov	Dec
Scott (°C)	⁻20	⁻40	⁻54	⁻57	⁻58	⁻58	⁻60	⁻60	⁻58	⁻51	⁻38	⁻28
Nord (°C)	⁻30	⁻30	⁻31	⁻24	⁻11	0	4	1	⁻9	⁻18	⁻23	⁻26

(a) Which of the two bases is colder in July?

(b) Which of the two bases is warmer in August?

(c) By how degrees is Scott base warmer than
Nord base in January?

(d) For how many months in the year is the temperature
at Nord base below zero?

(e) Which three months of the year do you think are summer
at Nord base?

(f) Which three months are summer at Scott base?

▽□● **A8** Materials which are gases at room temperature will freeze solid
if you make them cold enough.

For example, oxygen has a freezing point of ⁻219°C.

This table shows the freezing points of some materials
which are normally gases at room temperature.

Material	Argon	Helium	Hydrogen	Nitrogen	Neon	Oxygen	Radon
Freezing point (°C)	⁻189	⁻270	⁻259	⁻210	⁻249	⁻219	⁻71

Use the table to answer these questions.

(a) Which material has

(i) the lowest freezing point

(ii) the highest freezing point

(b) Which material has a freezing point 30 degrees
higher than oxygen?

(c) Which materials have freezing points 21 degrees
lower than another material?

▼■●

> ## Temperature trumps
>
> The cards for this game are on sheets 91 and 92.

B Temperature graphs

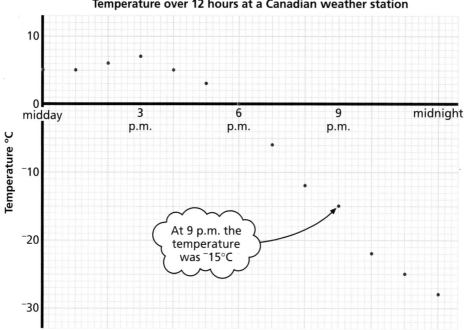

Temperature over 12 hours at a Canadian weather station

At 9 p.m. the temperature was ⁻15°C

B1 This graph shows the temperatures every hour from midday to midnight at a Canadian weather station.

(a) What was the temperature at 3 p.m.?

(b) When was the temperature ⁻12°C?

(c) What was the lowest temperature recorded?

(d) What time was the lowest temperature recorded?

(e) What was the highest temperature recorded?

(f) By how many degrees did the temperature drop between 8 p.m. and midnight?

B2 This graph shows the outdoor temperature during a night.

(a) What was the temperature at 10:30 p.m.?

(b) What was the lowest temperature?

(c) At what times was the temperature ⁻10°C?

(d) For how long was the temperature below ⁻5°C?

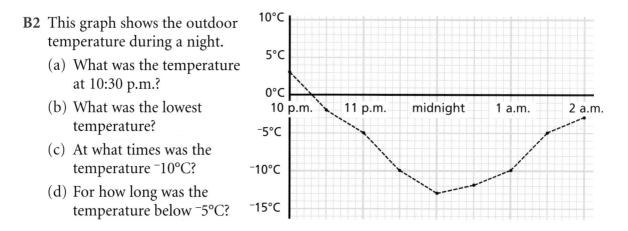

C Graph or table?

Arctic circle ➡

The table and the graph below both show the average monthly temperatures at two camps.
Sturge camp is on the Antarctic Circle.
Köge camp is on the Arctic Circle in Greenland.

⬅ Antarctic circle

Month	Jan	Feb	Mar	Apr	May	Jun	Jul	Aug	Sep	Oct	Nov	Dec
Sturge (°C)	⁻18	⁻35	⁻49	⁻51	⁻52	⁻54	⁻57	⁻57	⁻55	⁻45	⁻32	⁻27
Köge (°C)	⁻23	⁻21	⁻17	⁻17	⁻7	3	8	2	⁻4	⁻12	⁻18	⁻20

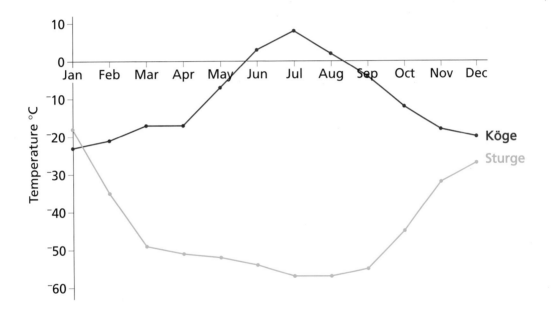

C1 (a) Use the table to find which camp is colder in July.

   (b) Now use the graph to answer the same question.

   (c) Which is easier to use for this question?

For each of the questions below, first use the **table** and then the **graph**.
Then say which was easier to use.

C2 Which camp is warmer in October?

C3 By how many degrees is Sturge camp warmer than Köge camp in January?

C4 Which three months are summer in Köge camp?

C5 Which three months are summer in Sturge camp?

D Changes ▽■●

Negative numbers have not always been thought to be 'proper' numbers.
Three hundred years ago many mathematicians simply ignored them.
We use '–' to mean two different things.

- There is ⁻2 (negative two) which can be a temperature or a point on a
  number line. The symbol '–' is raised slightly in this book.

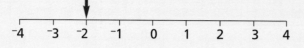

- There is also – 2 (subtract two) which only means something when it is
  a part of a calculation such as 7 – 2.

For discussion

How could you use a number line to help you
do calculations like these?

$$2 – 5$$

$$⁻2 – 5$$

$$⁻6 + 8$$

$$⁻6 + 3$$

For these calculations you may find it useful to make a sketch of the
number line.

D1 Copy and complete these.

 (a) ⁻2 + 3 =   (b) ⁻6 + 2 =   (c) ⁻8 + 8 =

 (d) ⁻8 + 10 =   (e) ⁻4 + 7 =   (f) ⁻1 + 6 =

D2 Copy and complete these.

 (a) 3 – 2 =   (b) 3 – 4 =   (c) ⁻5 – 4 =

 (d) ⁻3 – 3 =   (e) 0 – 4 =   (f) 4 – 7 =

 (g) ⁻7 – 4 =   (h) ⁻3 – 0 =   (i) ⁻5 – 2 =

D3 Copy and complete these.

 (a) ⁻3 + 2 =   (b) ⁻2 – 8 =   (c) ⁻5 + 4 =

 (d) ⁻6 – 2 =   (e) 3 – 7 =   (f) ⁻7 + 3 =

4
3
2
1
0
⁻1
⁻2
⁻3
⁻4
⁻5
⁻6
⁻7
⁻8
⁻9
⁻10
⁻11

D4 Write a calculation which fits each of these moves on a number line.

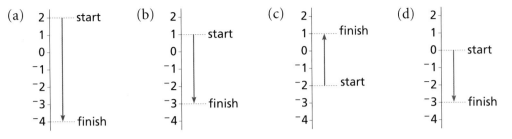

D5 Copy and complete these.

(a) $2 - ? = ^-1$ (b) $2 - ? = ^-2$ (c) $2 - ? = ^-3$ (d) $? - 7 = ^-5$

(e) $^-4 - ? = ^-5$ (f) $? - 5 = 2$ (g) $? - 10 = ^-2$ (h) $? - 4 = 4$

D6 Copy and complete these.

(a) $? + 3 = ^-5$ (b) $? + 4 = 2$ (c) $4 + ? = 7$ (d) $4 - ? = ^-7$

D7 Copy and complete these.

(a) $50 - 60 = ?$ (b) $^-30 - 50 = ?$ (c) $? - 60 = ^-100$ (d) $^-90 + ? = ^-10$

(e) $15 - ? = ^-100$ (f) $100 - ? = ^-21$ (g) $? - 18 = 42$ (h) $^-63 + ? = ^-15$

D8 Here are some sequences of numbers.

What are the next three numbers in each sequence?

Explain, in a few words, how you found the next three numbers.

(a) $10, 8, 6, 4, \ldots$

(b) $7, 5, 3, 1, \ldots$

(c) $40, 30, 20, 10, \ldots$

(d) $^-2, ^-4, ^-6, ^-8, \ldots$

(e) $^-12, ^-9, ^-6, ^-3, \ldots$

(f) Make up some sequences of your own.
Give them to someone to see if they can work out the next three numbers.

D9 Make some correct calculations (at least three) by putting any of the numbers below in the spaces.

$$^-4 \ + \ \ldots \ = \ \ldots$$

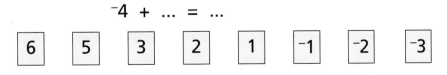

D10 Make at least three correct calculations by putting any of the numbers above in the spaces.

$$3 \ - \ \ldots \ = \ \ldots$$

D11 Work these out.

    (a) $^-5 + 2 + 8$ (b) $^-3 - 2 + 4$ (c) $4 - 6 + 8$ (d) $^-1 + 6 - 10$

    (e) $2 - 5 - 4$ (f) $^-5 - 1 - 4$ (g) $8 - 12 + 3$ (h) $^-4 + 1 - 7$

D12 The temperature inside a house is 15°C.

    The temperature outside is 20 degrees lower.

    (a) Which of these calculations do you do to work out
        the temperature outside?

| $^-20 - 15$ | $15 - 20$ | $^-15 - 20$ | $^-15 + 20$ |

    (b) Work out the result.

D13 Here are some questions and some calculations.
    Match a calculation to each question and work out the answer.

    (a) The temperature in a freezer is $^-20$°C.

        The temperature outside is 38 degrees warmer.

        What is the temperature (in °C) outside?

| $^-20 + 38$ | $20 - 38$ | $^-20 - 38$ | $^-38 - 20$ |

    (b) The temperature during the day in the desert is about 40°C.

        The temperature at night is 42 degrees lower.

        What is the temperature (in °C) in the desert at night?

| $^-42 + 40$ | $42 - 40$ | $^-40 - 42$ | $40 - 42$ |

    (c) The winter temperature at the South Pole is $^-60$°C.

        By summer it is 35 degrees warmer.

        What is the summer temperature, in °C?

| $^-60 - 35$ | $^-60 + 35$ | $^-35 - 60$ | $^-35 + 60$ |

    (d) The temperature in a warm room is about 20°C.

        The temperature in deep space is about 290 degrees lower.

        What is the temperature (in °C) in deep space?

| $^-290 + 20$ | $20 - 290$ | $290 - 20$ | $^-20 - 290$ |

E A mixed bag of negative numbers

▽□●

E1 The world record drop of temperature in 24 hours was at Browning, Montana, USA.

On 23/24 January 1916, the temperature fell from 7°C to ⁻49°C.

By how many degrees did the temperature fall?

E2 The temperature on the surface of the Moon, in the middle of its night, is about ⁻160°C.

By the middle of its day the temperature has risen by about 280 degrees.

What is the approximate temperature on the Moon at the middle of its day?

E3 Mercury, which is used in thermometers, freezes at ⁻39°C.

The temperature on a cold day is ⁻5°C.

How much would the temperature have to fall to freeze the mercury in a thermometer?

E4 The temperature of the air decreases steadily with height up to about 11 000 m.

This table shows the temperature of the air measured by a balloon as it rises.

Height of balloon (m)	2000	4000	6000	7000	8000
Air temperature (°C)	8	⁻4	⁻16	⁻22	⁻28

(a) What was the temperature drop between
    (i) 2000 m and 4000 m   (ii) 4000 m and 6000 m   (iii) 6000 m and 7000 m

(b) Use your answers to (a) to estimate the air temperature at
    (i) 5000 m   (ii) 9000 m   (iii) 1000 m

E5 Using nine of the digits 1, 1, 2, 3, 4, 5, 6, 7, 8, 9 once and once only, fill in the missing digits in these calculations and answers.

Can you find more than one way of doing this?

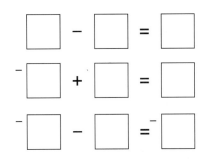

F The talent contest

Ellie's class have a talent contest.
The judges give points.

When they think a person is good they give scores like 4 or 6.

When they think a person is awful they can give negative scores.

The scores are added up each time.

Total
-2

What is the total score in each of these pictures?

F1 What is the total score in each of these pictures?

F2 Do these additions.

(a) $^-1 + ^-2 + 5$

(b) $1 + ^-1 + 3 + ^-4 + ^-1 + ^-1$

(c) $^-1 + ^-1 + ^-3 + 8 + 2$

(d) $3 + 2 + ^-6 + ^-2 + 8$

(e) $0 + ^-4 + ^-3 + 1 + 1$

(f) $^-6 + 2 + 7 + ^-3$

(g) $2 + 5 + ^-3 + 1 + ^-3$

(h) $^-2 + 8 + ^-3 + 1$

(i) $15 + ^-7 + 21 + ^-9$

Subtracting a negative number

Here are the points for Amanda.

The score of $^-5$ is taken off.

The total was 12. When $^-5$ is subtracted, it becomes 17.

$$12 - ^-5 = 17$$

F3 Jai got these scores.   **2** **$^-1$** **3**

(a) What is the total?

(b) The score of $^-1$ is taken away. What is the new total?

(c) Write a subtraction: $4 - ^-1 = \ldots$

F4 What subtraction does each pair of pictures below suggest?

(a)

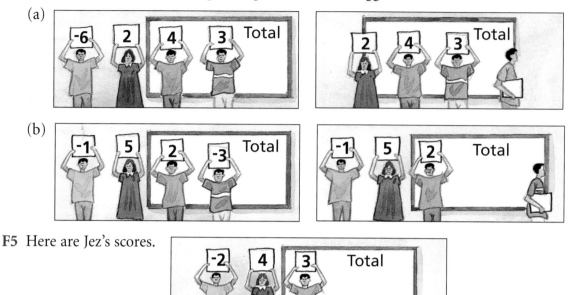

(b)

F5 Here are Jez's scores.

(a) Which of these is better, taking off ⁻2 or adding an extra score of 2?

(b) How could you work out 5 – ⁻2 in an easy way?

(c) What is an easy way to subtract negative numbers?

(d) Check your method works for subtracting other negative numbers.
    Explain your findings and give some examples.

F6 Work these out.

    (a) 7 – ⁻3
    (b) 15 – ⁻7
    (c) 36 – ⁻44

    (d) 203 – ⁻199
    (e) 0.7 – ⁻3.5
    (f) 3.57 – ⁻4.65

F7 Calculate these.

    (a) ⁻4 – ⁻9
    (b) ⁻21 – ⁻38
    (c) ⁻52 – ⁻31

    (d) ⁻105 – ⁻67
    (e) ⁻15 – ⁻221
    (f) ⁻3.5 – ⁻1.7

F8 Work these out.

    (a) 10 + ⁻2 – ⁻9 + ⁻7
    (b) ⁻9 + 11 + ⁻3 – 4

    (c) 28 – ⁻9 + ⁻7
    (d) 5.2 + ⁻1.3 – ⁻3.8

F9 (a) Subtract ⁻52 from ⁻51.
    (b) Subtract ⁻9 from the sum of ⁻8 and 10.

    (c) Add 21 to ⁻18 then subtract 5.
    (d) Add ⁻52 to 91 then subtract ⁻39.

F10 What calculations can you make with 4, 3, 1, 2, 5, ⁻, +, – and = ?

Magic squares

In a magic square,
    each row
      each column
      each diagonal
adds up to the same total.

8	1	6
3	5	7
4	9	2

F11 Make a magic square with these numbers:

   3   2   1   0 $^-1$ $^-2$ $^-3$ $^-4$ $^-5$

F12 Make a 4 by 4 magic square with these numbers:

   7   6   5   4   3   2   1   0

  $^-1$ $^-2$ $^-3$ $^-4$ $^-5$ $^-6$ $^-7$ $^-8$

What progress have you made?

Statement	Evidence
▼□○ ↓ I can write a negative number temperature.	1 Write the temperature 3 degrees below zero.
I can put a list of temperatures or numbers (some of which are negative) in order.	2 Write these temperatures in order, the lowest first. 0°C $^-6$°C $^-60$°C 18°C $^-18$°C
	3 Which temperature is higher, (a) 5 or $^-6$ (b) $^-5$ or $^-2$ (c) 0 or $^-10$
I can calculate final temperatures after a rise or fall.	4 The temperature in the evening is $^-4$°C. (a) By midnight it has dropped 6 degrees. What is the temperature at midnight? (b) The temperature at midday the next day is 26 degrees higher than it was in the evening. What is the temperature at midday?

Statement	Evidence

▽■●
↓ I can read a graph showing negative temperatures.

5 The graph shows the air temperature in a garden in Lincolnshire during 24 hours in January.

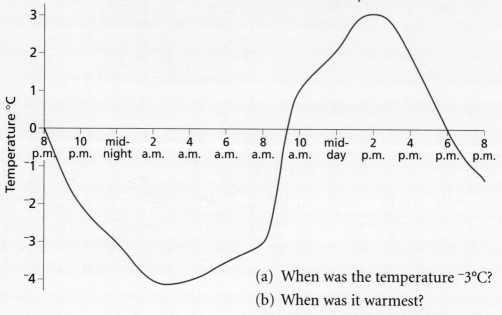

(a) When was the temperature ⁻3°C?

(b) When was it warmest?

(c) When was the temperature zero?

I can do simple calculations involving negative numbers.

6 Work these out.

(a) 5 − 8   (b) ⁻5 + 2

(c) ⁻6 − 8   (d) ⁻100 + 20

7 Fill in the missing numbers.

(a) ? − 5 = ⁻3

(b) 10 − ? = ⁻5

(c) ? − 1 = ⁻7

▽□● I can subtract a negative number.

8 Work these out.

(a) 7 − ⁻3   (b) 10 − ⁻8

(c) ⁻8 − ⁻3   (d) ⁻1 − ⁻6

Spot the rule

This work will help you

◆ recognise number patterns

◆ write rules for number patterns using words and algebra

A Finding rules

▼■●

This activity is described in the teacher's guide.

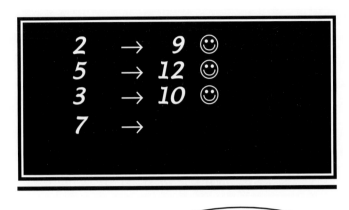

Brackets show what you do first.

A1 Look at the rule on the right. Work out what will happen to each of these numbers.

(a) 10 → ...   (b) 3 → ...

(c) 7 → ...   (d) 11 → ...

(e) 0 → ...   (f) 100 → ...

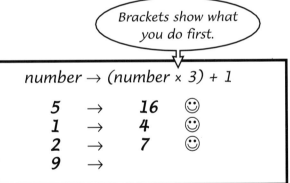

A2 This is Jane's rule: *number → (number × 2) – 1*

Choose five numbers of your own.
Show what happens to them with Jane's rule.

A3 Write down a rule of your own.
Choose three numbers and show what happens to each of them with your own rule.

What happens to each of these numbers when you use your rule?

(a) 10   (b) 8   (c) 0   (d) 100

B Using letters

*n is a short way to write **number**.*

B1 Copy and complete these tables.

(a)

number → number – 4
n → n – 4

7 →	3
12 →	...
20 →	...
4 →	...
... →	9
... →	20

(b)

number → number × 5
n → n × 5

3 →	15
8 →	...
2 →	...
10 →	...
... →	20
... →	30

(c)

number → number ÷ 2
n → n ÷ 2

10 →	...
16 →	...
22 →	...
0 →	...
... →	4
... →	6

B2 This is Suki's rule:

$$number → (number × 3) – 1$$

(a) Write Suki's rule using n.

Use her rule on these numbers.

(b) 10 → ...   (c) 4 → ...   (d) 1 → ...   (e) 11 → ...

B3 This is Karl's rule:

$$number → (number – 2) × 2$$

(a) Write his rule in a shorter way.

Work out what will happen to each of these numbers.

(b) 5 → ...   (c) 6 → ...   (d) 12 → ...   (e) 2 → ...

B4 Zeena began her game like this. ➡

(a) Which of these could her rule be?
(It might be more than one.)

number →	....
n →	....
4	→ 8

$n → n × 2$

$number → double the number$

$n → (n × 4) – 8$

$number → number + 4$

$n → (n × 3) – 4$

(b) Zeena writes another line in her table.
Now you can say which rule she is using.
Which one is it?

number →	....
n →	....
4	→ 8
3	→ 5

B5 Sam started a game like this.

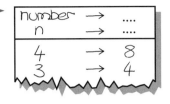

(a) Which of the rules in question B4 could be Sam's rule?

(b) Copy Sam's table and write in some numbers of your own.

B6 Shastra began a game like this. Find as many different rules as you can that could start like this.

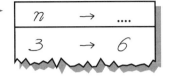

B7 (a) What is the rule for this game? Write it in words, and using $n \to$ ...

(b) Copy and complete the examples that have no answers.

16	→	8 ☺		8	→	...
22	→	11 ☺		4	→	...
100	→	50 ☺		12	→	...
18	→	9 ☺		3	→	...
				2	→	...
				1	→	...

B8 Copy and complete the tables for each of these rules.

(a)

n	→	$n \div 3$
12	→	...
21	→	...
30	→	...
3	→	...

(b)

n	→	$n \times 4$
3	→	...
5	→	...
1	→	...
10	→	...

(c)

n	→	$n \div 4$
8	→	...
12	→	...
20	→	...
2	→	...

B9 Daniel wrote this rule: $n \to (n + 1) \div 2$

What happens to each of these numbers?

(a) 5   (b) 11   (c) 1   (d) 19   (e) 4   (f) 0

B10 Sally wrote this rule: *number → (number subtract 2) then divide by 3*

(a) Write her rule in a shorter way.

What happens to each of these numbers?

(b) 8   (c) 14   (d) 5   (e) 32   (f) 2

C More shorthand

C1 Copy and complete these tables.

2n is a short way to write 2 × n.

(a)

n	→	n + 11
3	→	14
10	→	...
30	→	...
0	→	...
56	→	...
...	→	43

(b)

n	→	n ÷ 5
15	→	3
10	→	...
20	→	...
0	→	...
...	→	10

(c)

n	→	2n + 1
3	→	7
6	→	...
10	→	...
8	→	...
...	→	11

(d)

n	→	10 − n
3	→	7
8	→	2
4	→	...
9	→	...
5	→	...
...	→	3

C2 Write a rule of your own, using *n*.
On a separate piece of paper, write five numbers in a table,
and show what happens to them using your rule.

Show someone else your five pairs of numbers.
See if they can find your rule.

C3 Zahid began a game like this.

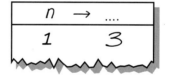

n	→	....
1		3

(a) Which of these could his rule be?
(More than one might be true.)

n → n + 2   n → 2n + 1

n → 3n   n → 4 − n   n → 4n − 1

(b) Later Zahid's game looked like this.
What was his rule?

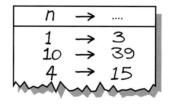

n	→	....
1	→	3
10	→	39
4	→	15

C4

1	→	6
5	→	26
10	→	51
8	→	41
2	→	11

(a) Find a rule for this table.
Write the rule using *n* → ...

What happens to each of these numbers?

(b) 4   (c) 20   (d) 25   (e) 0

C5 David's rule is $n \to 4n - 2$.

Copy and complete this table for David's rule.

$n \to$		$4n - 2$
3	$\to$	10
8	$\to$	...
4	$\to$	...
9	$\to$	...
...	$\to$	18

C6 Find the rules for each of these tables.
Write each rule in shorthand, using $n \to ...$

(a)

$n \to$		...
1	$\to$	5
10	$\to$	32
3	$\to$	11
12	$\to$	38

(b)

$n \to$		...
1	$\to$	5
10	$\to$	59
5	$\to$	29
25	$\to$	149

(c)

$n \to$		...
2	$\to$	7
10	$\to$	23
1	$\to$	5
100	$\to$	203

C7 Ann's rule is $n \to \dfrac{n}{4}$

This is shorthand for *number* $\to$ *number* $\div$ *4*.
Copy and complete this table for Ann's rule.

$n \to$		$\dfrac{n}{4}$
20	$\to$	5
12	$\to$	...
36	$\to$	...
100	$\to$	...
...	$\to$	8

C8 Danny chose this rule: $n \to \dfrac{n}{10}$

What will happen to each of these numbers?

(a) 20   (b) 50   (c) 25   (d) 5   (e) 0

C9 Write each of these rules as short as you can, using n.

(a) *number* $\to$ *5 × number*

(b) *number* $\to$ *number × 3*

(c) *number* $\to$ *(number × 2) + 4*

(d) *number* $\to$ *(number times 6) plus 2*

(e) *number* $\to$ *(number × 4) take off 1*

(f) *number* $\to$ *number add 12*

(g) *number* $\to$ *number divided by 2*

(h) *number* $\to$ *30 – (number times 2)*

(i) *number* $\to$ *number ÷ 6*

(j) *number* $\to$ *8 – (double the number)*

(k) *number* $\to$ *100 – (4 × number)*

(l) *number* $\to$ *half of number*

D Further rules

D1 Malik uses the rule $n \to n^2$.

n^2 is a shorthand for $n \times n$.

Copy and complete Malik's table.

n	$\to$	n^2
3	$\to$	9
10	$\to$	...
5	$\to$	...
...	$\to$	16

D2 Here are some more tables with rules involving n^2.
Look carefully at the first row in each table.
Make sure you understand how to use the rule.
Then copy and complete each table.

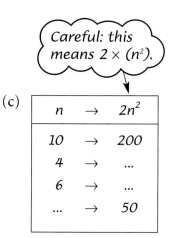

Careful: this means $2 \times (n^2)$.

(a)

n	$\to$	$n^2 + 1$
10	$\to$	101
5	$\to$	...
4	$\to$	...
...	$\to$	82

(b)

n	$\to$	$\dfrac{n^2}{2}$
10	$\to$	50
6	$\to$	...
8	$\to$	...
...	$\to$	12.5

(c)

n	$\to$	$2n^2$
10	$\to$	200
4	$\to$	...
6	$\to$	...
...	$\to$	50

D3 Can you spot the rule for each of these tables?
Write the rule in shorthand if you can.

(a)

n	$\to$	...
0	$\to$	10
5	$\to$	35
6	$\to$	46
10	$\to$	110
1	$\to$	11

(b)

n	$\to$	...
0	$\to$	0
10	$\to$	25
4	$\to$	4
8	$\to$	16
2	$\to$	1

(c)

n	$\to$	...
1	$\to$	0
3	$\to$	8
4	$\to$	15
8	$\to$	63
10	$\to$	99

(d)

n	$\to$	...
1	$\to$	2
3	$\to$	12
10	$\to$	110
0	$\to$	0
8	$\to$	72

D4 Work with a partner.

Think of a rule with n^2 in it.
Write down your rule so that it is hidden from your partner.

Your partner gives you a number, and you tell them
what answer your rule gives.

See how quickly your partner can find your rule.

What progress have you made?

Statement

Evidence

▼□○ I can use a simple rule in words.
↓

1 Copy and complete these tables.

(a)

number → number + 4		
3	→	...
6	→	...
10	→	...
...	→	8

(b)

number → number × 3		
2	→	...
4	→	...
10	→	...
...	→	9

I can test a rule.

2 Each of these rules goes with one of the tables A, B or C.

number → (number × 2) + 1
number → number + 3
number → (number × 3) – 1

Which rule goes with which table?

A

2	→	5
10	→	13
3	→	6
4	→	7

B

2	→	5
10	→	29
3	→	8
4	→	11

C

2	→	5
10	→	21
3	→	7
4	→	9

▼■○ I can find and write a rule.

3 Find a rule for the numbers in this table.

Write the rule down.

1	→	1
5	→	9
3	→	5
6	→	11

I can use simple rules with n in them.

4 For each of these rules, choose four numbers of your own and show what happens to them.

(a) $n \to n + 7$ (b) $n \to n \times 10$

▽■● I can use more complex rules with n in them.

5 (a) For these rules, choose four numbers of your own and show what happens to them.
   (i) $n \to 2n - 1$ (ii) $n \to 3n + 10$

(b) Write these rules using n.
   (i) number → (number times 2) plus 1
   (ii) number → (number × 4) take off 10

▽□● I can use rules with n^2 in them.

6 For each of these rules, choose five numbers of your own and show what happens to them.

(a) $n \to n^2 + 20$ (b) $n \to n^2 - 2$

16 Gravestones

This is about looking at data, displaying it and drawing conclusions.

The work will help you

◆ find information from a table

◆ draw a grouped frequency chart

◆ decide which sort of chart is best for the data

◆ use data to test a hypothesis

A What gravestones tell us ▼■●

Graveyards can be very interesting places.
Gravestones (if they can be read!) tell us

the person's name

the date when they died

how old they were

Gravestones have even been used to study the growth of moss!
The data on a gravestone tells us when it was put up.

Amy and Holly live in Manchester. They are working together on a history project.

It is about an old family called the Robinsons. Most of them are buried in St Mary's Church in Cheadle.

Amy and Holly went to the church and made a list of all the Robinson gravestones.

First names	Date when they died	Age
William	18 December 1832	54
John	24 January 1776	56
John Hanson	11 April 1798	4
Richard	29 July 1821	63
Jane	24 November 1827	68
Thomas	23 October 1790	69
Catherine	11 July 1793	71
Catherine	4 November 1757	2
Ann	26 August 1766	1
Frances	7 June 1772	6
Harriet	10 November 1813	1
Anne	16 March 1816	2
Hannah	5 March 1830	40
Martha	14 June 1846	57

A1 When was a Robinson first buried in St Mary's?

A2 For how many years were the Robinsons buried there?

A3 Amy says that most of the Robinsons seemed to die in winter. What do you think?

B Making a frequency table

Holly was interested in the ages at which people died.
She decided to make a **frequency table**.

Here is how she started …

Why is this not a good way to show the data?

It is better to **group** the ages.

Age (in years)	Tally	Frequency
0–9		
10–19		
20–29		
30–39		
40–49		
50–59		
60–69		
70–79		

Age (in years)	Tally	Frequency
1	ll	
2	ll	
3		
4	l	
5		
6	l	
7		
8		
9		
10		
11		
12		
13		
14		

B1 Copy and complete the grouped frequency table.
Does it show anything interesting about the ages at which people died?
Jot down anything you notice.

WILLIAM SKENELSBY.
DIED NOV.R 7TH 1775
AGED 118 YEARS

C Comparing charts

For work in pairs

These graphs were drawn on a computer.
Each graph shows the data about the Robinson graves.

C1 This is a frequency bar chart.

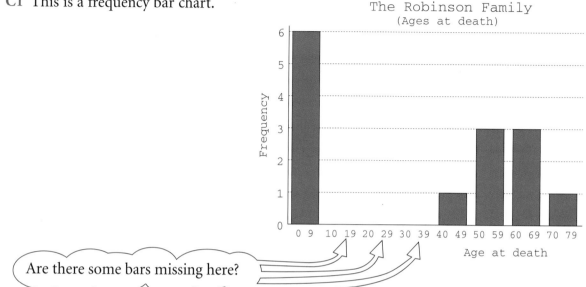

The Robinson Family
(Ages at death)

Are there some bars missing here?

C2 This is also a frequency bar chart, but the age groups are
marked differently.

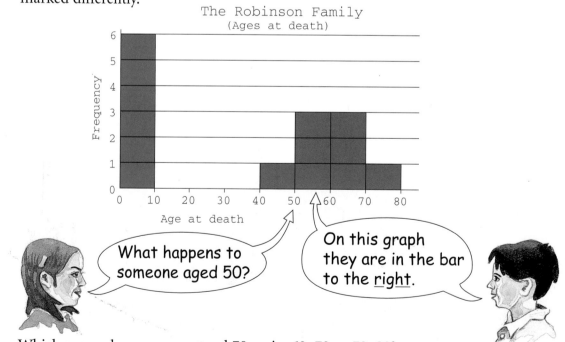

The Robinson Family
(Ages at death)

What happens to someone aged 50?

On this graph
they are in the bar
to the **right**.

Which group does someone aged 70 go in, 60–70 or 70–80?

184

C3 This is a pie chart.

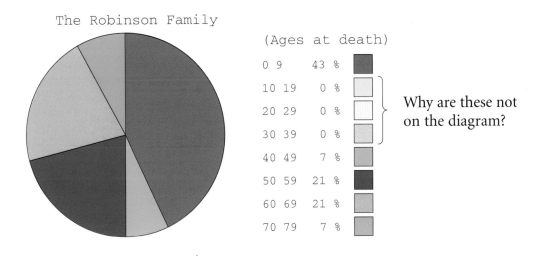

The Robinson Family

(Ages at death)

0 9	43 %
10 19	0 %
20 29	0 %
30 39	0 %
40 49	7 %
50 59	21 %
60 69	21 %
70 79	7 %

Why are these not on the diagram?

C4 Which chart best shows each of these?

(a) Almost half the Robinsons died before they reached ten years old.

(b) None of the Robinsons died between 10 and 39 years old.

(c) There are 14 Robinsons buried in St Mary's churchyard.

D Charts galore!

For class or group discussion

Computer software packages can draw lots of different charts.

Here are just a few.

They all look impressive, but which ones summarise clearly
the information in the grouped frequency table?

Age in years	0–9	10–19	29–29	30–39	40–49	50–59	60–69	70–79
Frequency	6	0	0	0	1	3	3	1

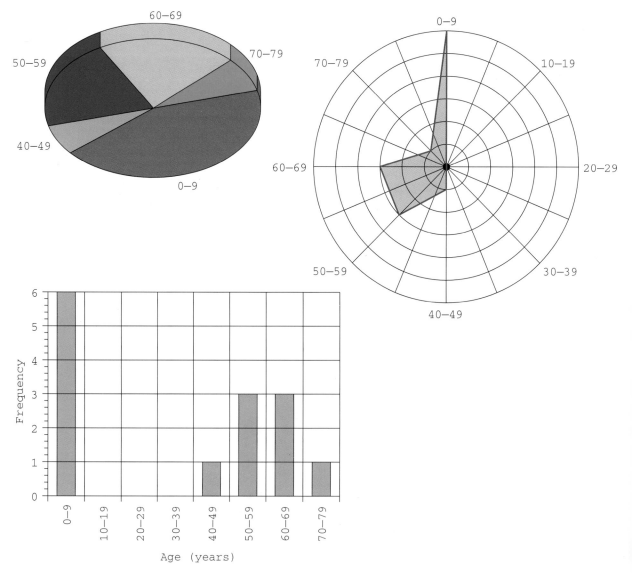

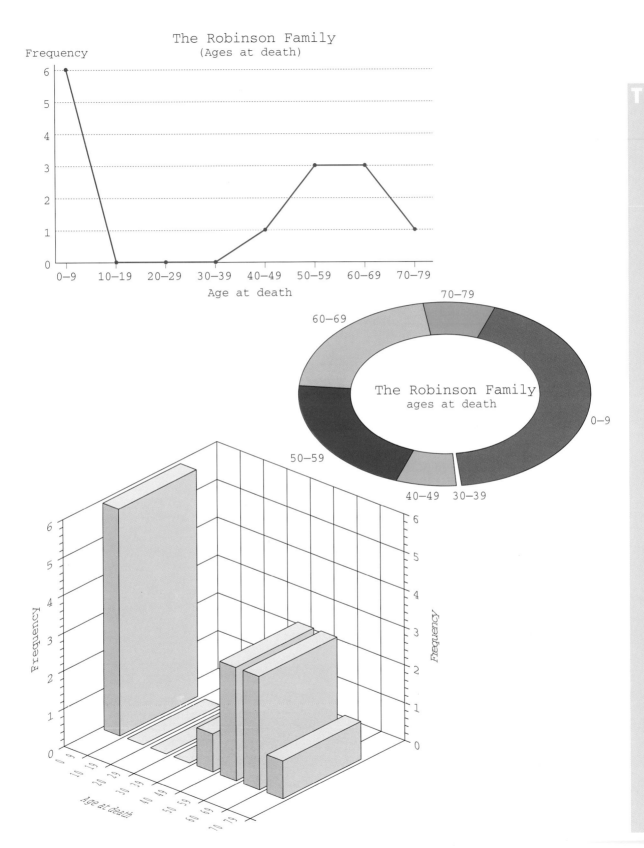

E Testing a hypothesis   ▽■●

Most of the Robinsons died during the winter months.
This *may* be true for other people living in the area at the same time.

The statement

> Most deaths in that area and at that time
> occurred during the winter months.

which we think *might* be true, is called a **hypothesis**.
To test the hypothesis and see if it is true, we need more data.

Here are some other hypotheses which the Robinson data suggests.

> More deaths occurred in the under
> 10s than in any other age group.

> If you reached the age of 20 there
> was a good chance of living to 60.

For group work

E1 Look back at the Robinson data on page 182.

Can you suggest a hypothesis of your own based on it?

E2 You need sheet 93.

It is a complete set of all the gravestone records for St Mary's.

Use these records to test the hypotheses above, and your own.

Write a report using suitable graphs to make your evidence clear.

> Here lyeth the bodie of
> John Millington Alderman of Stockport who
> departed this life on the first day of
> September MDCXCIV in the LIVth year of his age.
> Much regretted by all good men, for his singular piety.
> O death where is thy sting,
> O grave where is thy victory?

Challenge
When did John Millington die and how old was he?
Is it possible to calculate what year he was born?

F Every chart tells a story

Frequency charts are useful for displaying a lot of data.
They can make it easier to see what is going on.

▼□○ **F1** You need sheet 94.

▽■○ **F2** A group of people were each asked to pick
any number they wanted between 1 and 9.
The results are shown on this frequency bar chart.

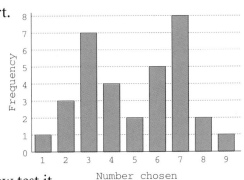

Numbers chosen by a group of people

(a) Which two numbers were
picked most often?

(b) How many people were
in the group?

(c) Looking at the chart what
hypothesis could you make
about people's choice of number?

(d) Plan how you could test your hypothesis. Now test it.

▽■○ **F3** You need sheet 95.

Table A gives the ages at which English rulers died.

(a) Make a grouped frequency bar chart. Use groups 0–9, 10–19, etc.

(b) Summarise in a couple of sentences what the chart tells you.

▽□● **F4** You need sheet 95.

Table B gives the time in minutes between eruptions of a
famous geyser called 'Old Faithful'. The measurements
were taken over two weeks.

(a) Make a grouped frequency chart.
Choose your own groups.

(b) Write a couple of sentences summarising what the
chart tells you.

(c) Imagine that you work in the Visitors' Centre.

A visitor just misses an eruption and wants to know
how long she will have to wait for the next.

What would you say?

189

What progress have you made?

Statement

▼□○ I can understand a frequency chart.
↓

Evidence

1 Bar chart showing when people died

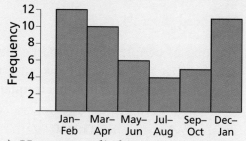

(a) How many died in January and February?

(b) How many gravestones were recorded?

(c) In which months did fewest people die?

I can make a grouped frequency table.

2 Here are some people's estimates of the length of a line, in cm.

6	11	10	19	12	10	14
30	12	14	21	12	17	6
24	16	19	15	12	21	7
11	13	14	13	15	22	14
14	13					

Copy and complete this grouped frequency table.

Estimate (cm)	Tally	Frequency
5-9		
10-14		
15-19		
20-24		
25-29		
30-34		

▽■○ I have tested a hypothesis.

Your work on testing one of the three hypotheses given on page 188.

▽□● I have made a hypothesis and tested it.

Your work on testing your own hypothesis based on the graveyard data.

190

Number patterns

This work will help you

◆ investigate number patterns
◆ understand prime numbers, square numbers, cubes and square roots

A Exploring a number grid   ▼■●

This activity is described in the teacher's guide.

The grid is on sheet 96.

A	B	C	D	E	F
1	2	3	4	5	6
7	8	9	10	11	12
13	14	15	16	17	18
19	20	21	22	23	24
25	26	27	28	29	30
31	32	33	34	35	36
37	38	39	40	41	42
43	44	45	46	47	48

1

Pick a number in column A and a number in column B.
Add your numbers together.
Which column is the result in?
Is this always true?

Investigate further.

2

Investigate the patterns made by multiples of 2, multiples of 3, and so on, in the grid.

3

Suppose the grid is extended downwards.
Can you predict the 30th number in column B?

How do you do it? Explain how to predict other numbers.

4

Can you predict which column 500 will be in?
What's the rule for predicting which column a number will be in?

5

Where are the prime numbers in the table?
Can you explain why some columns have no prime numbers in them?

B Dice numbers

You need a dice.

B1 (a) Put a dice on the table, with 5 on top.
   Can you say what number is on the bottom?
   Check to see if you are right.

   (b) If 3 is on top, what is on the bottom?

   (c) What is the rule for top and bottom numbers?

B2 For each of these dice,
   add up the numbers you can see,
   then add up the numbers you can't see.

(a)

Can see 2 + 4 + 1 = 7
Can't see .....

(b)  (c) (d)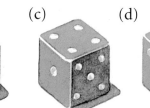

B3 (a) Can you hold a dice and see three
   numbers which add up to 11?

   (b) What other totals can you make like this?

   (c) What is the largest total you can make?

   (d) Can you make a total of 13?

I can see 3, 5 and 1.
The total is 9.

B4 Can you work out the total of **all** the numbers you can't
see in the pictures?

(a)   (b)   (c)   (d)

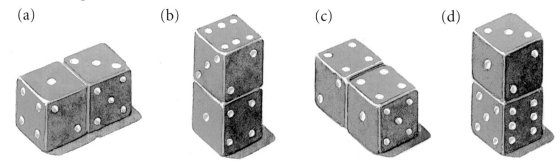

C Magic squares

This is a magic square.

If you add up each **row**
      or each **column**
      or each **diagonal**
you get the same total.

It is the 'magic total'.

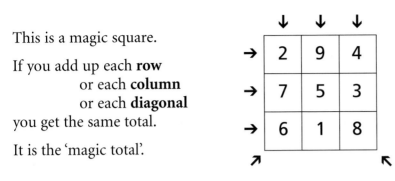

C1 What is the magic total of the square above?

C2 Copy and complete these magic squares.

(a)
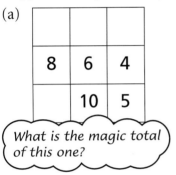

What is the magic total of this one?

(b)

6	11	4
10		

(c)

10		6
	7	
		4

C3 (a) Look at the magic square at the top of the page.
Add 5 to every number in it and make a new square.

(b) Is the new square also a magic square?
If so, can you explain why?

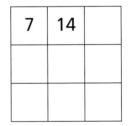

7	14	

C4 Copy and complete these magic squares.
Find the magic total first!

(a)

16	3	2	13
			8
9		7	
4	15		1

(b)

15		3	
	5		
14	11	2	
1		13	12

193

24 can make a **rectangle** pattern in different ways.

• • • • • • • • • • • •
• • • • • • • • • • • •

2 × 12

• • • • • •
• • • • • •
• • • • • •
• • • • • •

4 × 6

D1 Draw another rectangle pattern with 24.

D2 Here is one way to make a rectangle pattern with 20.
You can write it as 5 × 4 (or 4 × 5).

Can you find other ways?

• • • •
• • • •
• • • •
• • • •
• • • •

D3 Find as many ways as you can to make a rectangle pattern with

(a) 12   (b) 16 (A square counts as a rectangle.)

(c) 18   (d) 30

D4 Can you make a rectangle pattern with 17?
Are there any other numbers like 17? Give an example.

A number which can only make a single line pattern is
called a **prime** number.

2, 3, 5 and 7 are examples of prime numbers.

(1 is not a prime number. It won't even make a line.)

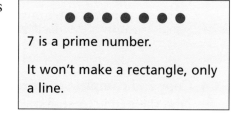

7 is a prime number.

It won't make a rectangle, only
a line.

D5 What are the next three prime numbers after 2, 3, 5 and 7?

D6 Why is it that all prime numbers except 2 are odd numbers?

D7 One number in each of these groups is prime. Which is it?

(a) 8, 9, 10, 11, 12   (b) 14, 15, 16, 17, 18   (c) 18, 19, 20, 21, 22

(d) 22, 23, 24, 25, 26   (e) 26, 27, 28, 29, 30   (f) 31, 32, 33, 34, 35

(g) 36, 37, 38, 39, 40

S Q U A R E
S Q U A R E
S Q U A R E
S Q U A R E
S Q U A R E
S Q U A R E **numbers**

Numbers which can make a square pattern are called **square numbers**.

4 is a square number. ⠶   So is **16**.

E1 What are the next two square numbers in this table?

1×1	2×2	3×3	4×4	5×5	?	?
•	•• ••	••• ••• •••	•••• •••• •••• ••••	••••• ••••• ••••• ••••• •••••		
1	4	9	16	25	?	?

E2 Continue the list of square numbers up to 100.

E3 Investigate the difference between each square number and the next.
(For example, the difference between 1 and 4 is 3.)
Is there a pattern?

Multiplying a number by itself is called **squaring**.

3×3 is called **3 squared**.
It is written 3^2 (say '3 squared').

E4 Work these out. (a) 4^2 (b) 5^2 (c) 11^2 (d) 20^2

E5 Rob thinks that 10^2 is 20. What has he done wrong?
Explain what he should have done.

E6 Work these out.
(a) $2^2 + 3^2$ (b) $7^2 - 4^2$ (c) $8^2 + 3^2$ (d) $6^2 + 5^2$ (e) $5^2 + 7^2 + 9^2$

E7 Write each number from 1 to 30 as the sum of square numbers
(as few as possible!).

$1 = 1^2$ $2 = 1^2 + 1^2$ $3 = 1^2 + 1^2 + 1^2$ $4 = 2^2$ $5 = 2^2 + 1^2$ ...

▽□● E8 Here is a way of splitting up 5^2 to make a pattern.

(a) What sum will you get if you split up 7^2 in a similar way?

(b) Can you work this out without adding?

$1 + 3 + 5 + 7 + \ldots + 37 + 39$

(c) Here are two more ways of splitting up 5^2.

$5^2 = 1 + 3 + 5 + 7 + 9$

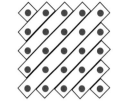

$5^2 = 1 + 2 + 3 + 4 + 5 + 4 + 3 + 2 + 1$

$5^2 = 1 + 8 + 16$

What are the sums you get when you split up 9^2 in each of these ways?

F 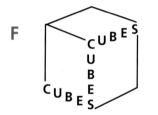   ▽■●

Imagine using small cubes to make a big cube 2 long, 2 wide and 2 high.

You would need 8 small cubes to make it, because $2 \times 2 \times 2 = 8$.

$2 \times 2 \times 2$ is called the cube of 2. It is written 2^3 (say '2 cubed').

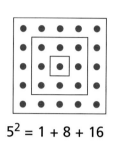

F1 (a) How many little cubes are needed to make a big cube 3 by 3 by 3?

(b) How do you write $3 \times 3 \times 3$?

F2 Work these out.

(a) $4^3 + 2^3$　　　(b) $5^3 + 5^2$　　　(c) $6^3 - 8^2$　　　(d) $10^3 - 7^3$

▽□● F3 Investigate the differences between consecutive cube numbers.
If you can't see any pattern, try looking at the differences between the differences!

▽□● F4 Jan made a huge cube from small cubes.
He broke it up and counted the small cubes he used.
He said 'I counted 3369 cubes, but I may not have been quite accurate.'
How many cubes did he actually use?

G Squa√e √oots

When you square a whole number, the result is a square number.
For example, $7^2 = 49$, which is a square number.

The number you started with is called the **square root** of the square number.
So the square root of 49 is 7.

The square root of 16 is 4, because $4^2 = 16$.

G1 Write down the square root of

(a) 9   (b) 25   (c) 100   (d) 64   (e) 1

The symbol for 'square root of' is $\sqrt{}$. We write $\sqrt{16} = 4$.

G2 Write down the value of   (a) $\sqrt{4}$ (b) $\sqrt{81}$ (c) $\sqrt{36}$

G3 Find the $\sqrt{}$ key on your calculator. Use it to calculate:

(a) $\sqrt{49}$ (b) $\sqrt{144}$ (c) $\sqrt{441}$ (d) $\sqrt{15\,129}$

G4 I think of a number and square it. The result is 961.
What number did I start with?

G5 The population of Belgium is about 9 000 000.

(a) Suppose everyone in Belgium stood in a square.
How many people would there be along each side
of the square?

(b) Estimate how long each side of the square would be.

G6 The population of the world is about 6400 million.
What sized square could all these people stand in?
Show clearly any estimates you made.

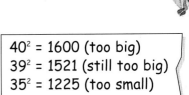

Imagine that your calculator does not have a square root key.
It is still possible to find square roots using multiplication and
trial and improvement.

G7 This is how Jade started to find the square root of 1369.
Finish off her work for her.

$40^2 = 1600$ (too big)
$39^2 = 1521$ (still too big)
$35^2 = 1225$ (too small)

G8 Use trial and improvement to find these.

(a) $\sqrt{729}$ (b) $\sqrt{1681}$ (c) $\sqrt{3249}$ (d) $\sqrt{848\,241}$

Only square numbers have square roots which are whole numbers.

20, for example, is not a square number.
20 is between 4×4 and 5×5, so $\sqrt{20}$ must be between 4 and 5.

G9 Without using the $\sqrt{}$ key, find the square root of 20 by trial and improvement, as accurately as you can. (How far you go depends on your patience, because the process goes on for ever! Even the $\sqrt{}$ key gives only an approximation.)

G10 Square roots occur in many formulas.
How far you can see depends on how high you are above the ground. The furthest you can see, in km, is

$$100 \times \sqrt{(\text{height in km above ground})}$$

(a) Jet planes fly at about 9 km high.
What is the furthest the pilot can see on the ground?

(b) A TV mast in South Dakota is 629 metres tall.
If you were brave (or mad) enough to climb to the top, how far could you see on the ground?

Test your skill at estimating square roots

Pick a number from the list below. They are all square numbers.

Use trial and improvement with a calculator to find its square root.
If you get it at your first trial: 10 points.
Lose 1 point for every extra trial.

You can play against someone else.
Take turns to pick a number.

2809	4489	7921	841	4356	3481
5476	5041	6724	8649	576	1849

True or false?

?

1 The square root of a number is always smaller than the number itself.

2 If you square any number, the result is always a larger number.

3 $2^2 = 4$ and $3^2 = 9$, so the square root of 6.5 (halfway between 4 and 9) must be 2.5.

H MISS NG NUMB RS

H1 (a) What are the next two numbers? **2, 5, 8, 11, 14, ..., ...**

(b) How did you work them out?

H2 Work out the next two numbers.
Write down the rule for working them out.

(a) **1, 8, 15, 22, 29, ..., ...**

(b) **31, 27, 23, 19, 15, ..., ...**

(c) **1, 12, 23, 34, 45, ..., ...**

(d) **63, 56, 49, 42, 35, ..., ...**

H3 Work out the missing numbers.

(a) **2, 8, 14, ..., 26, ..., 38**

(b) **5, 9, ..., ..., 21, ..., 29**

(c) **..., 11, 20, ..., 38, 47, ...**

(d) **36, 31, ..., ..., 16, 11, ...**

H4 One card is missing here.
What number is missing?

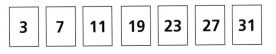

H5 Can you work out the missing numbers here?

(a) **..., ..., 20, 23, ..., ..., 32**

(b) **..., ..., 38, 30, ..., 14, ...**

H6 Two cards are missing here.
What numbers are missing?

H7 Work out the missing numbers.

(a) **7, ..., 13, ..., 19, ..., 25**

(b) **1, ..., 9, ..., ..., 21, ...**

I S, E, Q, U, E, N, C, E, S, ...

These are examples of number **sequences**.

2, 4, 6, 8, 10, ...
5, 9, 13, 17, 21, ...
23, 20, 17, 14, 11, ...

I1 (a) What is the next number in the first sequence?

(b) What is the rule for the sequence?

I2 (a) What is the rule for the second sequence?

(b) What is the rule for the third sequence?

I3 Work out the missing numbers and find the rule.

(a) **7, ..., 15, ..., 23, 27, ...**

(b) **1, ..., 7, ..., ..., 16, ...**

(c) **..., ..., 33, ..., 25, ..., 17**

(d) **44, ..., 34, ..., ..., 19, ...**

I4 All the sequences so far had simple rules. They all went up or down in equal 'jumps'. These are harder! Can you find the rule and work out the next number?

(a) **1, 2, 4, 7, 11, 16, ...**

(b) **3, 5, 9, 15, 23, 33, ...**

(c) **85, 82, 76, 67, 55, 40, ...**

(d) **2, 7, 14, 23, 34, 47, ...**

(e) **20, 19, 16, 11, 4, ...**

I5 Can you find the rule for the sequence printed across this page?

Challenge!

What are the missing numbers, and why?

(a) **1, 2, 4, 8, 16, 32, ..., ...**

(b) **1, ..., ..., 16, ..., 36, 49, ...**

(c) **2, 3, 5, 7, 11, 13, 17, ..., ...**

J Sequences in tables

J1 Check that you can see how the numbers 1, 2, 3, 4, 5, … are arranged in this table.

1	2	5	10	17	26
4	3	6	11	18	27
9	8	7	12	19	28
16	15	14	13	20	29
25	24	23	22	21	30
36	35	34	33	32	31

Imagine that the table goes on for ever.

(a) What is the sequence in the first column?

(b) How can you work out the numbers which will come in the first row?

(c) Find the rule for the diagonal sequence 1, 3, 7, 13, … .

J2

1	3	6	10	15	21	28
2	5	9	14	20	27	
4	8	13	19	26		
7	12	18	25			
11	17	24				
16	23				?	
22					?	

Check that you can see how the numbers 1, 2, 3, 4, 5, … are arranged here.

(a) What is the rule for the diagonal sequence 1, 5, 13, 25, … ?

Use it to work out the two numbers marked **?**.

(b) Investigate some other sequences in the table, and find their rules.

J3 Check that you can see how the numbers 1, 2, 3, 4, 5, … are arranged here.

Investigate the diagonal sequences, starting from 1 in the centre.

Can you work out the next two numbers on each diagonal without filling in all the numbers?

37	36	35	34	33	32	31
38	17	16	15	14	13	30
39	18	5	4	3	12	29
40	19	6	1	2	11	28
41	20	7	8	9	10	27
42	21	22	23	24	25	26
43	44	45	46	47	48	49

201

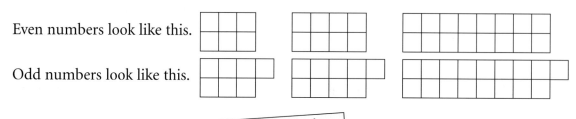

Even numbers look like this.

Odd numbers look like this.

Explain why it is that when you add two odd numbers the result is always even.

Numbers which follow one another, like 3 and 4 or 56 and 57, are called **consecutive**.

Explain why the sum of two consecutive numbers is always odd.

Is 1 + 2 + 3 + 4 + 5 even or odd?

Investigate the pattern of odd and even in
    1,   1 + 2,   1 + 2 + 3,   1 + 2 + 3 + 4   and so on.

Can you explain why the pattern occurs?

What progress have you made?

Statement

▼□○ I can investigate number patterns.
  ↓

Evidence

1

1	4	7	10	13	16	19	22
2	5	8	11	14	17	20	23
3	6	9	12	15	18	21	24

Choose a number in the second row and double it. Which row is the result in? Investigate doubling other numbers.

2 Work out the missing numbers.
Write down the rule for working them out.

(a) 5, 9, 13, 17, 21, …, …

(b) 43, 37, 31, 25, 19, …, …

(c) …, …, 24, 31, 38, 45, …

Statement	Evidence

I know about square numbers.

3 (a) Explain why 25 is a square number.

(b) What is the square of 4?

(c) Which square number is between 30 and 40?

I know what a prime number is.

4 (a) Explain why 13 is a prime number.

(b) Write down all the prime numbers between 20 and 30.

▽■○ I can find the rule for a sequence.

5 Find the rule and the next two numbers for each of these sequences.

(a) 52, 46, 40, 34, 28, ..., ...

(b) 1, 3, 7, 13, 21, 31, ..., ...

▽■● I know about the cubes of numbers.

6 Work out 4^3.

▽□● I understand what a square root is.
↓

7 (a) Explain why $\sqrt{144}$ is 12.

(b) Phil keeps confusing the square of 9 and the square root of 9. How would you explain the difference?

8 Use trial and improvement (not the $\sqrt{}$ key) to find $\sqrt{2819}$.

I can investigate number sequences.

9 Investigate some sequences here.

25	16	9	4	**1**	2	5	10	17	
	24	15	8	3	6	11	18		
		23	14	7	12	19			
			22	13	20				
				21					

Review 4

▼□○ **1** You can make several rectangle patterns from 36. Here is one.

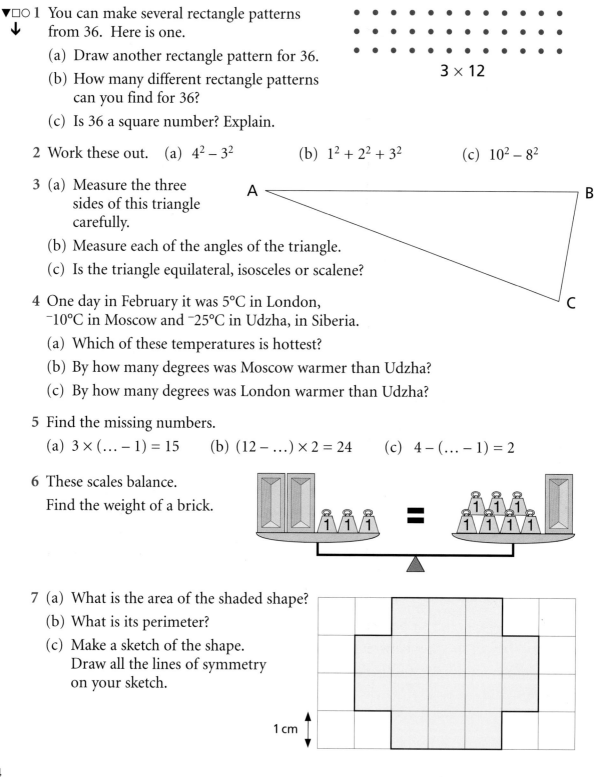

3×12

    (a) Draw another rectangle pattern for 36.

    (b) How many different rectangle patterns can you find for 36?

    (c) Is 36 a square number? Explain.

2 Work these out.   (a) $4^2 - 3^2$ (b) $1^2 + 2^2 + 3^2$ (c) $10^2 - 8^2$

3 (a) Measure the three sides of this triangle carefully.

    (b) Measure each of the angles of the triangle.

    (c) Is the triangle equilateral, isosceles or scalene?

4 One day in February it was 5°C in London, ⁻10°C in Moscow and ⁻25°C in Udzha, in Siberia.

    (a) Which of these temperatures is hottest?

    (b) By how many degrees was Moscow warmer than Udzha?

    (c) By how many degrees was London warmer than Udzha?

5 Find the missing numbers.

    (a) $3 \times (\ldots - 1) = 15$ (b) $(12 - \ldots) \times 2 = 24$ (c) $4 - (\ldots - 1) = 2$

6 These scales balance. Find the weight of a brick.

7 (a) What is the area of the shaded shape?

    (b) What is its perimeter?

    (c) Make a sketch of the shape. Draw all the lines of symmetry on your sketch.

1 cm

▽■○ **8** Here are sketches of two triangles.

(a) Draw each of the triangles accurately.

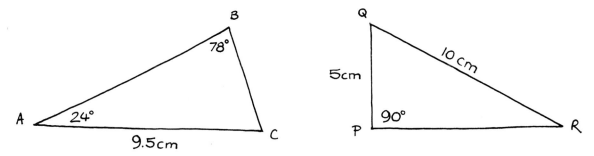

(b) Measure the sides and angles that are not marked on the sketches.

(c) Are both triangles scalene?
Describe the type of each triangle as accurately as you can.

9 Work these out.

(a) ⁻5 + 7   (b) ⁻3 − 4   (c) ⁻6 + 2   (d) ⁻11 + 5

(e) 4 − 9   (f) ⁻2 + 8   (g) ⁻3 − 7   (h) ⁻5 + 7 − 3

10 (a) Find a rule for continuing this sequence: 2, 7, 12, 17, ...

(b) Write the next three numbers in the sequence.

11 (a) Find a rule for continuing this sequence: ⁻21, ⁻17, ⁻13, ⁻9, ...

(b) Write the next three numbers in the sequence.

12 Draw a sketch of this shape.

(a) By splitting your sketch up, work out the area of the shape.

(b) Work out the perimeter of the shape.

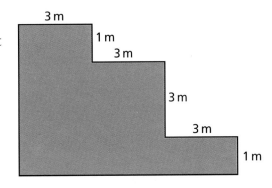

13 Draw a rectangle with a perimeter of 32 cm and an area of 48 cm².

14 Write down:

(a) a square number between 40 and 50   (b) a cube number between 100 and 200

(c) a prime number between 25 and 30   (d) a prime number between 90 and 100

(a) Find an approximate rule connecting these pairs of measurements.

Foot length (cm)	Index finger length (cm)
27.5	8.3
21.5	6.5
35.3	10.7
23.8	7.2
22.8	6.9

    (b) Siobhan's index finger is 9.5 cm long. About how long would you think her feet are?
(Give your answer to the nearest 0.5 cm.)

    (c) Liam has a foot length of 30 cm. About how long is his index finger?
(Give your answer to the nearest 0.1 cm.)

16 Calculate the angles a, b, c, d, e and f.

35°   72° b a c f d e 18°

17 Work these out.

    (a) $^-3 + ^-8$ (b) $^-3 - ^-8$ (c) $^-8 - ^-3$ (d) $3 - 8$

    (e) $8 - ^-3$ (f) $3 - ^-8$ (g) $^-3 + 8$ (h) $^-8 + 3$

18 Copy and complete these.

    (a) $5 - (3 - ...) = 2$ (b) $5 - (3 - ...) = ^-2$ (c) $5 + (3 - ...) = ^-2$

    (d) $5 + (3 - ...) = 2$ (e) $5 - (3 + ...) = 2$ (f) $5 - (3 + ...) = ^-2$

19 **Without using a calculator**, work these out.

    (a) $\sqrt{(5^2 - 3^2)}$ (b) $\sqrt{(13^2 - 5^2)}$ (c) $(10 - \sqrt{16})^2$

20 Find a rule for continuing each of these sequences
Copy each sequence and fill in the missing numbers.

    (a) $^-4, ^-1, ..., ..., ...$ (b) $2, ..., ^-12, ...$

    (c) $8, 4, 2, ..., ..., ...$ (d) $1000, 100, 10, ..., ..., ...$

21 Draw a rectangle with a perimeter of 33 cm and an area of 50 cm².

22 Work out the area of each of these.

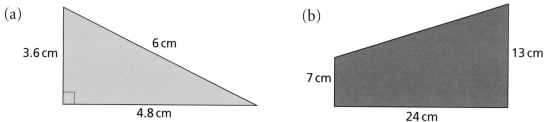

(a) 3.6 cm, 6 cm, 4.8 cm   (b) 7 cm, 13 cm, 24 cm

More challenging questions

23 (a) How much is a mile of 1p coins worth?
(A mile is 1.6 kilometres.)

(b) Make a rough measurement of how
many times your heart beats each minute.
About how long would it take your heart
to beat a million times?

> **BILBROOK SCOUTS**
> Mile of pennies
> **P L E A S E   H E L P**

24 There are 5 squares in this 2 by 2 grid.

(a) How many squares are there
in a 3 by 3 grid?

(b) How many squares are there in
a 10 by 10 grid?

25 Three people were asked to continue the sequence 2, 4, 6, …
Here are their answers.

John: 2, 4, 6, 8, 10, 12, 14, 16, …

Paul: 2, 4, 6, 10, 16, 26, 42, 68, …

Sue: 2, 4, 6, 12, 14, 28, 30, 60, …

Explain what rule each person might be thinking of
to get their sequence.

26 (a) In this problem, each letter
stands for a different digit.
What does each letter stand
for?

$$\begin{array}{r} S\,E\,N\,D \\ +\ M\,O\,R\,E \\ \hline M\,O\,N\,E\,Y \end{array}$$

(b) What does each letter stand
for here?

$$\begin{array}{r} C\,R\,O\,S\,S \\ +\ R\,O\,A\,D\,S \\ \hline D\,A\,N\,G\,E\,R \end{array}$$

27 One evening there was a power cut from 11 p.m. to 11:30 p.m.
After the power cut, Imran's electric clock started up again
immediately, but the hands went backwards at half their usual speeds.

When Imran switched on the radio the next morning,
the time given by the radio agreed with the time shown
on his clock.

What time was it?

28 (a) The ball goes in at A and falls to B. How many different ways can it fall from A to B?

(b) How many different ways can the ball fall from C to D?

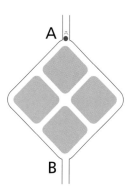

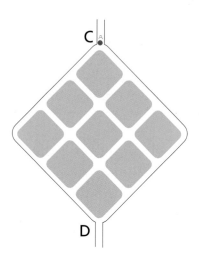

29 22 and 23 are called consecutive numbers because they follow one another when we write numbers in order.

(a) Pick any two consecutive numbers. Multiply them together.
Repeat with another pair of consecutive numbers.
Is the answer even or odd? Explain why.

(b) 7, 8 and 9 are consecutive numbers. Multiply them together.
Check that the result divides exactly by 6.
Try it with 8, 9, 10 and 12, 13, 14.
Explain why the result is always true.

(c) Pick **four** consecutive numbers. Multiply them together.
What is the highest number your answer can always be divided by? Explain why.

30 There are five children in the Stone family.

On Monday, four of them go to a film. Their ages add up to 38.

On Tuesday, four of them go skating. Their ages add up to 35.

On Wednesday, four go to a disco. Their ages add up to 36.

On Thursday, four go swimming. Their ages add up to 36.

On Friday, four go to a concert. Their ages add up to 38.

On Saturday, four go to a football match. Their ages add up to 39.

No child goes out on all six occasions.

What are the ages of the children?